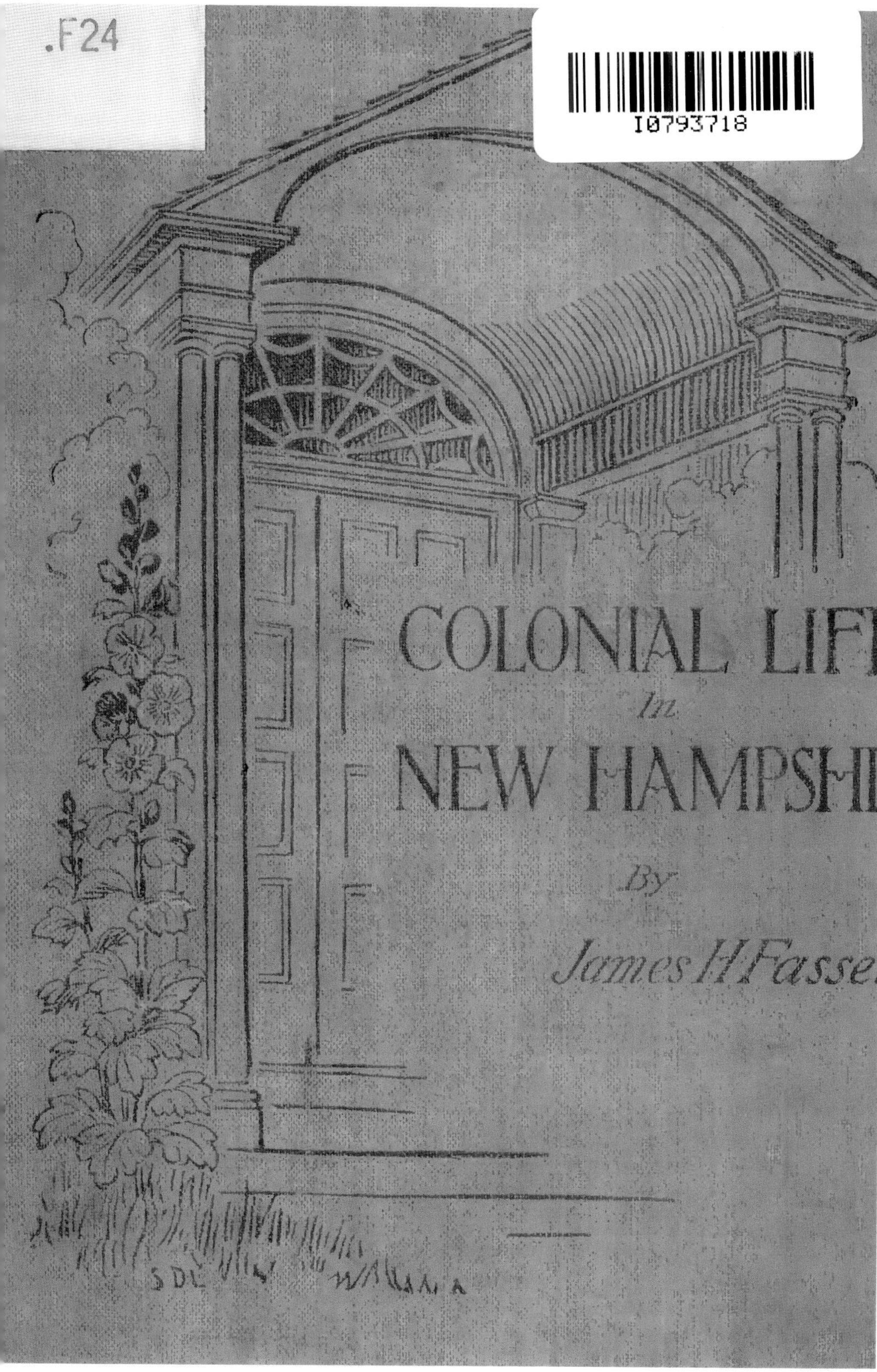
COLONIAL LIF
In
NEW HAMPSHI
By
James H Fasse

Marula
An imprint of Arcadia Publishing

Colonial Life in New Hampshire
by James H. Fassett

A Marula Historical Reprint
Originally published in 1899

Published by Arcadia Publishing
Charleston SC

ISBN 978-0-7385-9456-9

Printed in the United States of America

For all general information contact Arcadia Publishing at:
Telephone 843-853-2070
Fax 843-853-0044
E-mail sales@arcadiapublishing.com
For customer service and orders:
Toll-Free 1-888-313-2665

Visit us on the Internet at www.arcadiapublishing.com

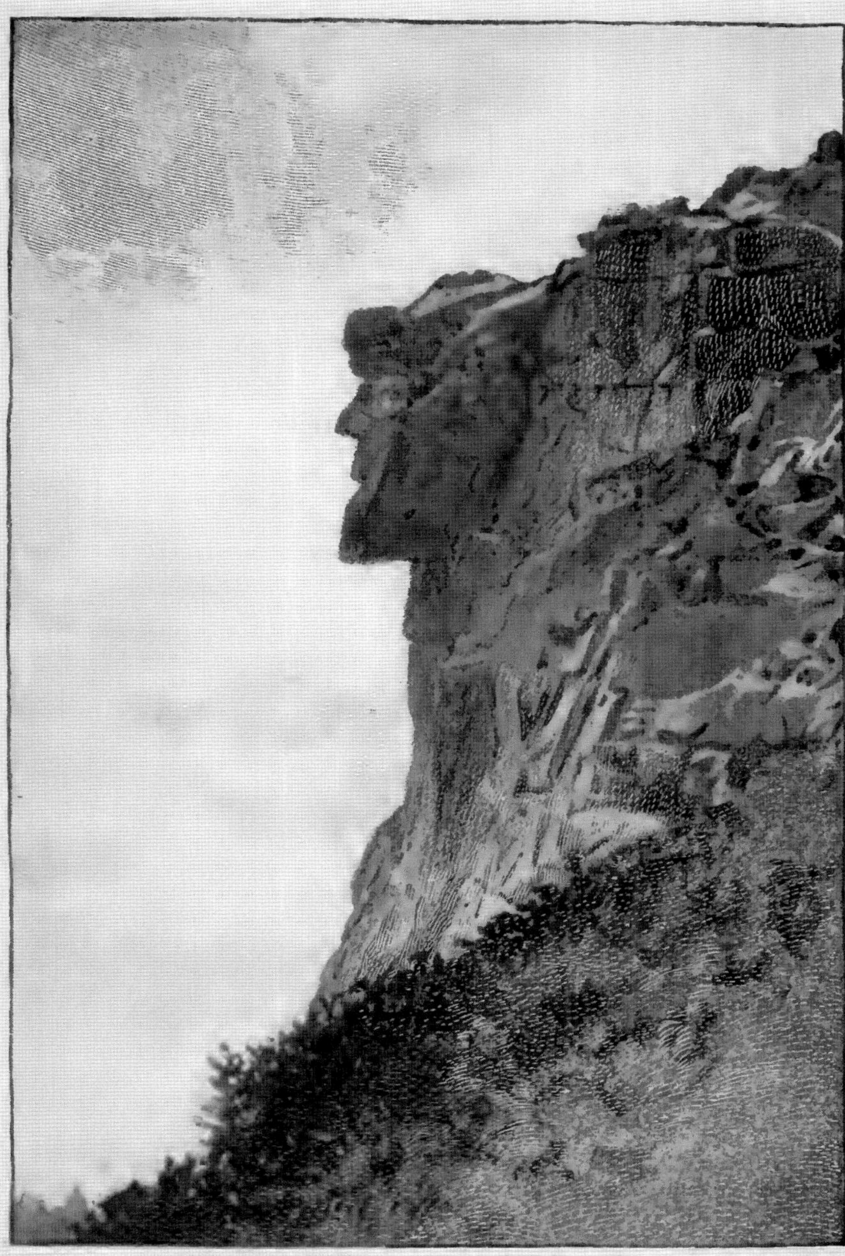

The Old Man of the Mountain.

COLONIAL LIFE

IN

NEW HAMPSHIRE

BY

JAMES H. FASSETT

BOSTON, U.S.A.
GINN & COMPANY, PUBLISHERS
The Athenæum Press
1899

PREFACE.

It is the belief of the author that the aim of all teachers of history should be to cultivate and foster in the minds of children a fondness for historical reading, rather than the mere memorizing of historical facts. In order to best accomplish this purpose, the child's interest should first be awakened by the historical associations of places with which he is familiar. He should be told the legends and stories of the town or city in which he lives, and at the same time carefully led to see their connection with the broader historical life of the country. Following the stories of local interest, the early history of the colony, with its accounts of the struggles and hardships endured by the early settlers, should be developed. This method will tend not only to broaden and intensify the child's interest in historical reading, but will give to him some conception of the value of his birthright as an individual of the state and of the nation.

In writing the "Colonial Life of New Hampshire," it was thought best, for many reasons, to treat the subject topically rather than in the chronological order. In the separate chapters, however, events have been narrated, so far as possible, in their natural order.

The author acknowledges his indebtedness to the local histories of New Hampshire towns; Belknap's "History of New Hampshire"; Chase's "History of Dartmouth College"; and Batchellor's editions of New Hampshire State Papers.

CONTENTS.

LIST OF ILLUSTRATIONS.

COLONIAL LIFE

IN

NEW HAMPSHIRE.

CHAPTER I.

EARLY SETTLEMENTS.

The First Settlers.—During the summer of 1603 two small vessels commanded by Captain Martin Pring sailed into what is now Portsmouth Harbor and explored Piscataqua River for some distance. Pring was much pleased with the thickly wooded hills and the rich lowlands along the river banks, and, upon returning to England, gave such an account of the country that many Englishmen of influence and wealth became interested in this part of the New World.

Settlement at Pannaway.—In the year 1622 Mr. David Thompson obtained from the Grand Council of Plymouth a grant of land consisting of six thousand acres, the site of which was to be chosen by himself.

With a company of colonists, he sailed in midwinter in a ship called the "Jonathan of Plymouth," and arrived at the Piscataqua in the spring of 1623. He chose for his place of settlement a location near the present city of Portsmouth, and soon completed a stone house large enough for himself and his followers. Thompson remained at this place, which was called Pannaway, several years, during which time he traded with the Indians for furs, and caught and salted fish which were found in great quantities off the coast. Shortly after the settlement was established he was visited by the renowned Miles Standish of the Plymouth Colony. This small settlement remained and flourished, although its leader in the year 1626 moved to the colony of Massachusetts.

Settlement at Dover. — About the time of the settlement at Pannaway a small company under the leadership of Mr. Edward Hilton built several log cabins near the present town of Dover, with the intention of establishing a trading-post. It was customary for the Plymouth company to demand that before any grant was made some settlement should be started to indicate the good faith of the persons who desired the land. Accordingly, Hilton brought to the notice of the Plymouth company the improvements which he had made on the Piscataqua, and in consideration of these, the company in the spring of 1630 granted him six thousand acres.

The Company of Laconia. — In 1629 the Grand Council of Plymouth gave to Sir Ferdinando Gorges, Captain John Mason, and seven other gentlemen a tract of territory near Lake Champlain, to which province they gave the name of Laconia, "on account of the great lakes therein." These men imagined that Lake Champlain lay about ninety miles from the coast, and that the head waters of the Piscataqua were but a few miles from this region. They therefore hired the buildings which were erected seven years before by David Thompson, and made them a basis of supplies for expeditions to this country which they supposed was to be so easily reached. After struggling for two years to find a direct route to Laconia, all efforts were abandoned.

During this time, the colonists had noticed the many advantages which the region about the Piscataqua offered for commerce and fishing, and the Company of Laconia in 1631 obtained a grant to this section; but this grant in no way conflicted with the land previously given to Hilton. For a number of years the company continued under the leadership of Captain Walter Neale; but as nothing was done toward reclaiming the wilderness, and as their returns were meagre, the company soon disbanded.

Mason at this time bought the shares of two of his associates, and shortly before the surrender of the Grand Patent of the Company of Plymouth, procured a new grant of land in this section, which he called New Hampshire. But the name New Hampshire was not commonly used until 1679, when the colony was made a royal province. Mason persevered in his idea of settling this territory, and sent over many colonists with farming tools and cattle. He also set up two sawmills. Mason died in 1635, and for a time his widow managed the estate through her agent, Francis Norton. Finding that the expenses exceeded the returns, she soon severed all connection with the colony and left the settlers to shift for themselves as best they could.

Founding of Exeter. — In the year 1638 the Reverend John Wheelright, a man of remarkable intellect and of great independence, came from the Massachusetts Colony with a band of followers and settled at Exeter. He had been banished from Massachusetts on account of his belief in the religious teachings of Mrs. Anne Hutchinson a woman of great power, who profoundly stirred the theological minds of her time. A year after the founding of Exeter a code of laws was agreed upon, which formed the first written constitution of any New Hampshire settlement. The next year the colonists along the Piscataqua River entered into a similar constitution in order to protect themselves against "sundry mischiefes and inconveniences." Thus the little settlements acknowledged their mutual dependence for law and order upon a written agreement which was more or less binding for all their people.

Grants by Massachusetts. — The early towns along the Merrimac River for a long time were supposed to be under the jurisdiction of Massachusetts, and grants were made under the authority of that colony. Of these towns, Dunstable was the earliest to be settled, but many others soon obtained charters from Massachusetts. This land was practically given to the settlers, but a nominal fee known as "quitt rents" was reserved by the authorities. In some instances the payment consisted of one ear of Indian corn for a rental of ten years. Usually a number of settlers combined and asked for the charter of a township, which was afterwards surveyed and divided among them, generally by lot.

Massachusetts finally had so many petitions presented for lands that she granted not only townships, but lines of towns, which were so situated as to effectually protect the frontier settlements. In the southern part of the state four lines were granted in the form of a quadrilateral extending west from Dunstable to Northfield, Massachusetts; from that place north along the east side of the Connecticut; thence east to Penacook (Concord), and from Penacook south to Dunstable. Only two of these sides were really settled under this arrangement, — the north side, where they were numbered from one to nine, and the west side, where they were numbered from one to four: it was from this fact that Charlestown was originally known as Number Four.

Conflicts with the Indians. — During the early years of the colony the settlers found the Indians well disposed, and these friendly relations were maintained for a long time. They traded with each other to mutual advantage. The Indians furnished many things to the whites, who in turn gave the Indians many articles which they were unable to make.

Gradually, however, misunderstandings began to arise. As the settlements spread, the Indians found themselves pushed farther and farther back toward the west, where they were checked by the powerful Iroquois. They could not understand the white men's ideas of the ownership of land, nor could they comprehend the strict laws of the settlers or the crimes for which they were sometimes punished. They saw their hunting grounds and garden spots turned into farms and villages, and, becoming desperate, resolved to regain their lands from the settlers. In consequence, many expeditions were made against the exposed settlements. In these attacks the Indians were aided by gifts of arms and ammunition from the French in Canada, and therefore our forefathers were scarcely less bitter toward the French than toward the savages themselves.

The Indians practiced the same cruelties upon the

whites that they were accustomed to inflict when fighting with each other. Always after a successful attack the captives who were not capable of traveling were put to death, and the others were taken to Canada, where they were either held for ransom or sold as slaves. It is estimated that during one year ten per cent of the men in New Hampshire were killed by Indian raiders. Men carried their flintlock guns with them everywhere,—into the fields on week-days and into the meeting-houses on Sundays. To protect their log cabins, they built around them high fences of upright logs, which were sharpened and driven close together into the earth. In order to attack people within, the Indians had to expose themselves in climbing over these palisades. In addition, every community had at least one blockhouse, which was a sort of fort built large enough to hold several families. The first story was constructed like a log cabin, but the second was so built that it projected out beyond the first. By this means the attacking

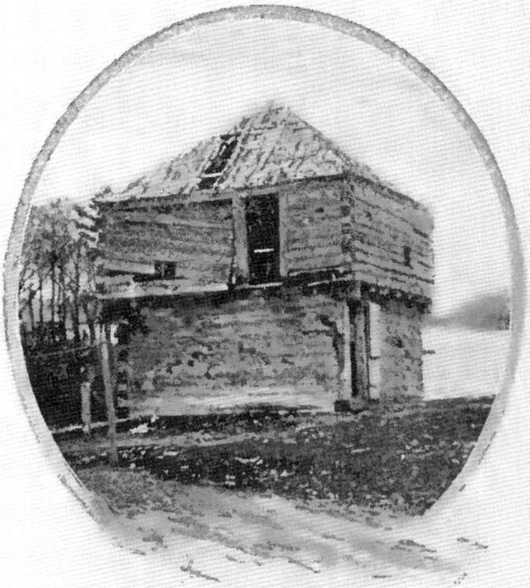

Blockhouse.

party could be fired on from above and driven from the walls, which would otherwise protect the Indians without as much as they did the settlers within.

Death of Major Waldron (1689). — During these troublesome times in New Hampshire the exposed settlements in Massachusetts were attacked by Indians under the command of a powerful chief named Philip, but after several massacres the savages were overcome and their leader was killed. A large number of Philip's people came to the tribes in the southern part of New Hampshire, where they attempted to stir up a warlike spirit. This reached the ears of the authorities in Boston, and a company of soldiers was sent to stop the threatened uprising. Upon reaching Dover they found two or three hundred Indians entertained by Major Waldron whom the savages considered their fast friend. Among this number there were several of King Philip's Indians whom the soldiers wished to take prisoners at once, but Waldron advised them to wait until the next day, when he would arrange a sham fight, and the Indians, being unarmed, could be taken without resistance. This was done, and, not suspecting any surprise, they were easily captured. All, however, were released, with the exception of King Philip's old soldiers, who were brought captive to Boston. Eight of them were afterwards convicted of murder and hanged, while the rest were sold as slaves.

The Indians never forgave Major Waldron his treachery, and while still pretending friendship were quietly laying plans for revenge. On the evening of June 27, 1689, two squaws applied at each of the garrison houses in Dover for permission to sleep. A chief named Mesandowit was also entertained at Major Waldron's. While they were at supper the Indian quietly asked Waldron, "What would you do if the strange Indians come?" Waldron, with confidence in the strength of his defense, replied, "I can assemble a hundred and fifty men by lifting my finger."

During the night the squaws unbarred the doors of the blockhouses, and, at a signal, the Indians who were waiting outside rushed in and began their terrible work. Major Waldron, although eighty years old, grasped his sword and for a time beat them back, but finally was knocked down by a blow from behind. The savages lashed him to his armchair, placed it on a table, and told him to judge Indians now as he had done before. A number of them owed him money for goods, and each of these drew his knife across the old man's breast, crying, "Thus I cross out my account!" while others taunted him with his treachery. At last, fainting from the loss of blood, he fell to the floor and the house was set on fire.

Attacks upon the Settlement at Oyster River. — Two months later in the same year a large body of Indians came down the Oyster River, with the intention of attacking the garrisons at that place. They first killed a party of eighteen persons belonging to Huckins' garrison, as they were going to their morning devotions, and then attacked the house, in which were only women and children. For some time the savages were heroically beaten off by the efforts of two young boys, who poured a continuous fire upon them and wounded several. At length they set fire to the house, but even then the boys would not surrender until the Indians had promised to spare the lives of all the inmates. They broke their word, however, and all the younger children were killed, while the rest were carried away as captives.

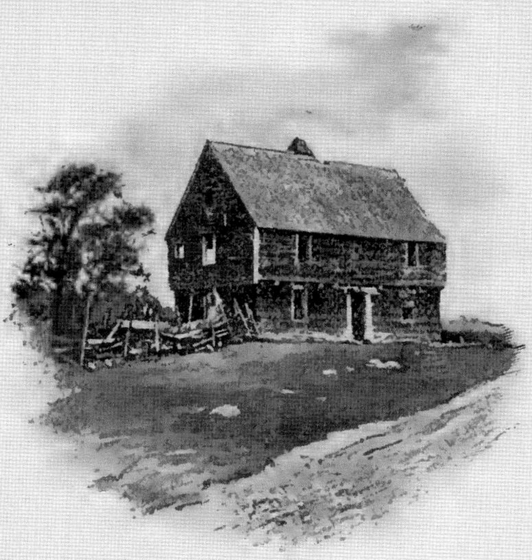

Garrison House.

During the summer of 1694, under the leadership of Sieur de Villieu, a company of two hundred fifty Indians made a general attack upon the fourteen garrison houses at this settlement on Oyster River. In the encounter which followed, five of the blockhouses fell into the hands of the enemy, and their inmates were either horribly murdered or sold into slavery in Canada. The others successfully resisted the attacks, and several of the Indians were killed.

A brave man named Bickford, being forewarned of the advance, sent his wife and children down the river in a boat, and determined to defend his home single-handed. The Indians endeavored to persuade Bickford to surrender, but he refused with scorn all their offers. In order to deceive them and make them think that they were opposed by a strong force, he changed his coat and his hat many times and fired from different loopholes about the fortress. He also gave stirring commands to an imaginary band of defenders. The Indians were completely deceived by his stratagem, and after a short time the entire force withdrew and left the solitary man in possession of the home he had so nobly defended.

Bravery Shown by Women. — The attitude which the women assumed during these trying times is one of which New Hampshire may be justly proud. Strong of body and keen of intellect, they were ever ready to help their husbands in the protection of their families. When it was necessary for the men to be absent they did the work in the fields and cared for the live stock. When fighting was to be done they could always be relied upon to handle the flintlock as ably as the men in defense of their homes. Too much honor, indeed, cannot be paid to the wives of our forefathers.

Among the captives taken at the attack upon Dover was Sarah Gerrish, a little seven-year-old girl, granddaughter of Major Waldron. At the end of a most fatiguing journey she arrived with her captors in Canada. After some time she was purchased by a wealthy French lady and placed in a nunnery; but later she was ransomed and returned to her parents, who had given up all hope of seeing her again.

On the 22d of March, 1690, the village of Salmon Falls was attacked by a band of Indians and utterly destroyed. Thirty of the people were killed and as many more taken to Canada as captives. One of these, Robin Rodgers, was burned at the stake as punishment for attempting to escape during the journey. Mehitable Goodwin, another of the captives, had a most terrible experience. The savage into whose charge she had been given, annoyed by the crying of her child, which was so small that she carried it in her arms, snatched it away and killed it before her eyes. Upon arriving in Canada she was sold as a slave and kept five years, at the end of which time she was enabled to return to her friends, who had mourned for her as dead.

During the spring of 1706 the Indians attacked a cabin near Oyster River and killed all of its inmates.

They then made an attack upon a blockhouse near by. As it happened, there was not a man in the fort at the time. The women, however, not at all daunted, loaded their guns and prepared for a stubborn fight. That the Indians might think they were men, they undid their hair and allowed it to hang loosely over their shoulders. They also shot from different loop-holes, in order that the savages might be deceived as to their numbers. The fire which they poured upon the attacking force was so sharp and so accurate that after a short time the Indians withdrew, having lost many of their best warriors.

Colonel Winthrop Hilton.—During the year 1710 the settlements of New Hampshire lost one of their bravest defenders in Colonel Hilton. While busily at work peeling bark from mast trees, he and his work-men were ambushed by a party of Indians; at the first fire Hilton and two of his men were killed, but the remainder of the party were able to make their escape.

Many stories are told of the prowess of Hilton. The following account, although related many years afterwards, is doubtless true.

Previous to the trouble with the Indians Colonel Hilton had always been very friendly with them. On many occasions he had been of assistance to the savages by furnishing them food and shelter and by protecting them from being cheated in trade with unscrupulous whites.

After the outbreak of the wars, however, the Indians found that they were constantly being thwarted in their plans by Hilton's wisdom and cunning. Finally, one of the chiefs, who had formerly been his particular friend, decided that Hilton must die, and for this purpose ten of his best warriors were picked out and instructed by the old chief not to return without him, alive or dead. They came upon him as he was weeding corn not far from the blockhouse, with his rifle resting against a stump at some little distance. Quietly the Indians took advantage of the situation, and, having crept between Hilton and his gun, demanded that he accompany them.

Hilton immediately saw that he was securely caught, and, putting a pleasant face on the matter, treated the whole proceeding as a good joke of his old friend the chief. He chatted with his captors in the most unconcerned manner, asking about their families and their success in trapping. In this way they tramped several miles, until they reached a deserted log house which the Indians appropriated. As they were so strong in number they took no special precaution against their captive. They securely barred the only door, and, after setting their guns together in a corner, each one proceeded to roast his meat before the open fire.

Meantime Hilton was constantly talking with them, and finally asked permission to examine their guns. This being granted, he took up the guns one by one, and as he did so commented on the good points of their "kill-deers." The Indians did not notice, however, that as he set them back each one was cocked and ready for firing.

A most singular contest now took place. One man matched himself against ten; with the utmost coolness and quick as lightning, one Indian after another fell under his accurate aim. The Indians rushed upon him, but were driven back by tremendous blows from the stock of his gun, and as they reeled back more guns were fired and each time an Indian was killed.

Thus the struggle continued until but one red man was left alive. He succeeded in unbarring the door and in making his escape. Hilton, with the ten guns upon his shoulders, marched in triumph toward his home, and on the way was met by a company of settlers who had started out for his rescue.

The Dunstable Massacre. — An Indian raid which turned out most unfortunately for the settlers at Dunstable, New Hampshire, occurred in September, 1724. One morning Nathan Cross and Thomas Blanchard, citizens of the town, crossed the Nashua River and began their usual work of making turpentine from the pine trees which abounded in this region. The day being rainy, they placed their luncheon and their guns in the hollow trunk of a fallen tree. While busy at work and wholly unsuspicious of an attack, they were surrounded by a large body of Indians and forced to surrender. The savages then cut the hoops of the barrels of turpentine, and, having done as much mischief as possible, took the two men with them as captives up the west bank of the Merrimac.

The neighbors, becoming frightened at their long absence, crossed the river in search of them. They easily found from the signs that Blanchard and Cross had been captured, and one of the brightest of the party judged, as the turpentine from the barrels had not yet ceased flowing, that it had not been long since the capture was effected.

This man, Farwell by name, counselled the others to take a circuitous route and by marching rapidly, to get ahead of the Indians and thus surprise them. Their leader, however, thinking Farwell's advice arose from cowardice, urged them to follow directly on the path of the Indians, and started off, saying, "I shall take the direct path. If any one of you is not afraid, let him follow me."

They had journeyed hardly three miles when the Indians, expecting this pursuit, fell upon them from an ambuscade and killed them all, with the exception of Farwell, who had cautiously kept in the rear, and thus was able to escape after a hot pursuit. He made his way back to the settlement and reported the result of the struggle. This was an exceedingly hard blow to the little town of Dunstable, which could ill afford at this time to lose eight of its most valued protectors.

On the next day a strong party went to the scene of conflict, and the bodies of the slain were brought home. They were all interred in one grave, and an old headstone in the cemetery back of the school-house at South Nashua may now be seen marking the spot of their burial. The two captives were taken to Canada and were finally ransomed. After many years, when these men returned to their homes, they found the remains of two guns still lying in the hollow tree where they had been placed so long before. The settlers became furious at these repeated attacks and made many expeditions against the savages, but, as the latter were far more familiar with the ways and paths of the forest, very few of these were successful.

Headstone in South Nashua Cemetery.

Lovewell's Fight (1725). — John Lovewell of Dunstable, was a man particularly well fitted for waging Indian warfare. His sagacity and knowledge of woodcraft made him a formidable opponent to the cunning of the savages. Two successful expeditions were made under his charge. On the first, the scouting party killed one Indian and captured a boy, and on the second, they surprised and killed a body of eight Indians, who, armed with new guns and plenty of ammunition, were evidently on their way to attack and to plunder the settlements.

Encouraged by this success, Lovewell was enabled to raise a body of men for the purpose of attacking a village of Pequakets under the noted chief Paugus. When about thirty miles distant from this village the company halted a few days, in order to make a rude fort to which they might retire in case of defeat. One morning after the completion of the fort, as they were marching in Indian file along the shore of a small lake, an Indian was seen a little way in front. Suspecting that he was placed there for the purpose of leading them into an ambush, they quietly put off their packs and cautiously advanced. When within range, the Indian was fired upon and killed, but not until he had seriously wounded Captain Lovewell.

Meantime, a large body of Indians under Paugus, who had been following them for two days waiting a favorable opportunity to attack, had seized the packs and by counting them, learned that the white men were fewer in number than they had supposed. They quietly concealed themselves and waited for the return of the settlers. As Lovewell's men came forward the Indians fired, and then followed for more than eight hours a severe battle. From behind trees and rocks both Indians and whites watched keenly for one who should expose any part of his body.

After several hours of this kind of fighting the rifles of Chamberlain, one of the white men, and of Paugus, the Indian chief, became fouled. They both, as it happened, crept to the pond to wash their guns at the same time. Then came a trial to see which could get his gun cleaned and loaded first. Both worked with equal rapidity, and their guns were loaded at the same time. But in those days guns had to be primed, that is, a little powder was poured into a small pan, which caught the fire from sparks struck by the flint. Fortunately, Chamberlain's gun had so large an opening leading from this pan to the barrel of his gun that by striking the stock a sharp blow the pan would fill itself with powder, while Paugus had to pour some into his from his powder horn. This gave Chamberlain an advantage. Aiming his gun at Paugus, he fired and killed him, but he had indeed very little time to spare, for the bullet from Paugus' gun cut a hole in his cap.

At dusk the Indians withdrew. Then it was found that there were only nine men out of the thirty-four who were uninjured. The Indians, with twice as many at the beginning of the fight, had less than twenty unharmed. This fight, although not a decisive victory, was very disheartening to the savages.

It is impossible to describe the terrible sufferings

of the wounded while endeavoring to return to the settlements. One man, who owing to his wounds was unable to walk and had to be left, asked them to load his gun and place it by his side in order that he might shoot one more Indian before being scalped.

Expedition to Louisburg (1745). — As a key to their possessions in Canada, the French, at an enormous expense, had built and fortified Louisburg. The walls of the fortress were constructed of solid masonry forty feet thick at the base, twenty-five feet high, and surrounded by a deep moat.

There were three things which led the colonists to make an expedition against this fortress. In the first place, it was understood that there was much dissension among the soldiers at the fort, leading almost to mutiny. Second, for a long time their commerce had suffered because French vessels had used the harbor at Louisburg as a perfectly safe place from which to make their sallies and to which they could retreat in case of attack. And, finally, they were led by popular indignation, which had been aroused through the harsh treatment of English prisoners who had been kept at Louisburg. So strong was the feeling concerning this expedition that men of all trades and professions, even clergymen, volunteered. Colonel William Pepperell of Kittery was put in command.

Louisburg was considered impregnable by the French. They had one hundred sixty-one cannon, seventy-six swivels, and sixteen hundred men. They thought that two hundred men could defend it against a force of five thousand; yet it proved that sixteen hundred men were not able to hold it against four thousand Yankees with only eighteen guns and three mortars.

The French were, indeed, astonished to see a New England army approaching, because, besides the massive walls, there were deep marshes to be crossed, over which it seemed impossible to transport artillery. A New Hampshire colonel, however, solved the problem. He built sledges of wood, on which the guns were placed, and the men, often knee-deep in mud, drew them through the marshes by means of straps over their shoulders.

One of the most conspicuous officers of this campaign was Colonel William Vaughn of Portsmouth. He conducted the first column through the woods and when within sight of the city saluted it with three cheers. Later, with a detachment of but thirteen men, he captured and held a battery of thirty guns, although it was attacked by a force of French, outnumbering his own little company ten to one.

These successes, together with the capture of the French ship "Vigilant," which was laden with military stores for the relief of the garrison, led the French commander on June 15, 1745, to surrender Louisburg, which was probably the strongest fortress in the world.

When news of the victory was received the people went fairly wild with rejoicing and offered to invade Canada; but England was afraid to encourage a knowledge of war in her colonists, fearing lest they would realize their own strength and rebel against the home government. This victory, however, showed the Americans what a band of resolute men could do against a powerful enemy.

When the treaty was made between France and England, Louisburg was given back to France, much to America's disgust; but it was not to remain long in her possession.

French and Indian Attack upon Charlestown. — In the spring of 1747 Captain Phineas Stevens, with a party of thirty men, occupied a deserted fort, then called Number Four, but now known as Charlestown, New Hampshire.

He had hardly time to put the fort in repair before it was attacked by a large party of Indians, under the leadership of Monsieur Debeliné. The dogs at the fort fortunately warned the garrison of the Indians' approach, so that the defenders were able to take every precaution. The attack was carried on sharply, and many men were lost on both sides. The Indians tried by every means in their power to burn the fort. They set the adjoining buildings on fire and shot flaming arrows upon the roof of the garrison house, but through the watchfulness and daring of the inmates their efforts were not successful.

For two days the attack continued, when the French officer asked for a parley, at which he ordered Stevens to surrender the fort, stating that if this were done he would consider the Americans prisoners of war, but if his demands were refused all should be killed. To this calm proposal Stevens replied that, until compelled, he would not surrender the fort which had been intrusted to him. The French officer returned, "Go and see if your men dare fight any longer, and give me a quick answer." Stevens then told the Frenchman that his men were fully as anxious to fight as he was himself, and that they would continue to hold the fort. Angered at this reply, coming as it did from so small a body of men, the Indians, led by their French commander, made a furious charge, attacking three sides of the fort at the same time. The brave garrison, realizing that to be captured meant death by torture, fought desperately. After a sharp hand-to-hand encounter the Indians were driven back, but not until they had suffered the loss of many warriors.

The next day, after asking for another parley, two Indians came forward to say that if Stevens would sell them some corn they would retire. Stevens replied that he could not sell them provisions, but that he would give them five bushels of corn for every English captive for whom they should leave a hostage until the captives could be brought from Canada. At this reply a few shots were fired at the fort and the attacking forces withdrew. The news of this successful resistance was received with great rejoicing at Boston, and Stevens obtained merited praise for his stubborn defense. Sir Charles Knowlton, who was in Boston at the time, presented Stevens with a costly sword, and it was from this same Sir Charles that Number Four was afterward called Charlestown.

Kilburn's Defense. — During the spring of 1755 an Indian named Philip called at the cabin of John Kilburn, who, with several others, had settled near the present town of Walpole. Philip, who could speak a few words of English, came into the cabin, and, after lighting his pipe with a coal from the fireplace, asked Kilburn's wife to give him a piece of flint for his gun; upon receiving this he disappeared. It happened that Kilburn had reason to visit the settlements lower down on the river, and he learned that the Indian had also called there and had asked for flints. This fact aroused suspicion that the Indian was acting as a spy and caused the settlers to be doubly cautious in all their movements. To add to this alarm, news was brought by a friendly Indian, sent from Governor Shirley of Albany, New York, that four or five hundred Indians were about to start from Canada for the purpose of destroying all the settlements along the Connecticut. The settlers took every precaution in their power to meet this expected attack. Doors and windows were strongly barred, and the houses were fortified as thoroughly as possible.

The first attack fell upon Kilburn. As he and a man named Peak were returning from their morning's work with their two sons, they discovered the legs of several Indians through the underbrush which skirted the meadow. Without waiting to investigate further, they ran for the cabin and securely fastened the door. The Indians, seeing that their intended ambuscade was discovered, did not attack them at once, but crossed the mouth of Cold River, where they placed themselves in ambush to surprise Colonel Bellows (for whom Bellows Falls, Vermont, was named), who was working with his men a short distance east of this place. In this they were disappointed, for the dogs belonging to Bellows' men gave them warning, so that after a sharp encounter they were able to elude the Indians.

The savages, balked in this attempt, returned to Kilburn's cabin. Philip, the treacherous spy, approaching the house, cried out:

"Old John, young John, I know you. Come out here; we give good quarter."

"Quarter!" shouted Kilburn, "quarter! you black rascals; begone, or we 'll quarter you!"

At this reply a general volley was fired at the cabin which riddled the roof, but the thick logs which formed the sides offered an effectual resistance. Our small band of defenders prepared for a stubborn fight. Powder was poured into hats that it might be gotten at more readily. In addition to the four already named, Kilburn's wife and his daughter Hattie aided much in the defense.

During the first part of the engagement the women were kept busy reloading the extra guns which by good fortune they possessed. Very unfortunately, during the fight their store of bullets ran out. The pewter dishes and spoons, however, were quickly melted and run into bullet moulds, and when these were exhausted the quick-witted women thought of a method of obtaining lead from the enemy. While there was a lull in the firing they hung heavy blankets from the ridgepole. The bullets, retarded by passing through the roof, were stopped by the blankets and fell harmlessly to the floor. These they quickly gathered up and melted over again.

Several times the Indians tried to force open the door by means of a battering ram. Ten or a dozen of the bravest would lift a huge log upon their shoulders and rush with it against the door of the cabin. Nothing but the stoutest oak could withstand these tremendous blows. This method of attack, however, exposed the Indians to a heavy fire from the cabin, and, after a few trials, they were forced to give up the idea of breaking in the door. The fight continued unceasingly until sundown, when, baffled by the stubborn resistance which they had so unexpectedly encountered, they withdrew, but not until many Indians had been killed.

Destruction of the Indian Village of St. Francis.—The best known and most cordially hated of all Canadian governors was Count Frontenac, who came to this country first in 1672. Ten years later he was withdrawn from his governorship, but when war was declared against Great Britain in 1689 he was again given command.

Count Frontenac instigated many Indian raids against the English settlements, and furnished the Indians with guns and ammunition. He even went so far as to collect a number of Indian tribes in a village called St. Francis, in order that he might have them constantly at hand as a menace to the English colonists.

In September, 1759, nearly a hundred years after St. Francis was founded, Sir Jeffrey Amherst determined to teach these Indians a lesson, and for the purpose gave Major Rogers command of a company of two hundred men, with orders to lead them against this village.

Starting from Crown Point, Rogers, with his troops, passed down Lake Champlain in boats. On the fifth day after leaving Crown Point a keg of powder accidentally exploded, killing a number of men and seriously wounding several others, who had to be conducted by a guard back to the fort. This unfortunate affair reduced the force from two hundred to one hundred forty-two men. Arriving at Missiscoe Bay, Rogers concealed his boats in the bushes, together with sufficient provisions for the return journey. On the second day of their march he was overtaken by the two men who had been left on guard at the lake. They had traveled in great haste to inform him that a party of four hundred French and Indians had discovered the boats and started in pursuit. The fate of the expedition looked dubious; either he must give up the attack, or outmarch his pursuers. He determined on the latter course, and his little band pushed on rapidly. On the 4th of October, at eight o'clock in the evening, they came in sight of the town of St. Francis, where the Indians, entirely unsuspecting, were having a grand dance. During the night, Rogers placed his men around the village, and at break of day they began the attack. The Indians were completely surprised and made little resistance. The white men, having found poles, scattered through the village, to which had been fastened many scalps of English women and children, were beside themselves with anger. Between two and three hundred Indians were killed. The whole village had become enriched by the sale of English scalps to the French government and from the plunder which had been captured on their many raids. Over a thousand dollars in money was found, a silver image weighing ten pounds, and large quantities of wampum and supplies. The entire place was burned, and at eight o'clock on the morning of the assault Rogers was in retreat. During the march he was attacked from the rear by a small band of Indians, who shot several of his men. Favored by dusk, he formed an ambuscade on his own track, and fell upon and killed the Indians who followed him.

For about ten days the detachment kept together, and then it was thought best to divide into small parties which could march more rapidly toward some of the English settlements. Through lack of provisions, the men suffered extremely, but Rogers, with a majority of his force, finally reached Number Four. This expedition made a deep impression on the savages and caused a feeling of insecurity which they never before had experienced.

Capture of Canada. — The next year, 1760, Sir Jeffrey Amherst appeared before Montreal, and its commandant surrendered the city, together with the whole of Canada. The Peace of Paris was brought about in 1763, by which all the French and Indian wars were made a thing of the past. Hereafter the settlers were allowed to possess their homes and pursue their trades in peace.

CHAPTER II.

THE INDIANS OF NEW HAMPSHIRE.

New Hampshire, abounding as it does in mountains, rivers, and beautiful lakes, seemed an ideal spot for the Indians. The woods were full of game and the rivers of fish. It is no wonder that the Indian was loath to give up his right to this place which nature had made so beautiful and which was particularly well fitted for his savage mode of life.

The Algonquin Race. — Throughout the state were many small tribes or families, each of which was composed of kinsmen. In times of great danger, however, these small families united and chose a leader, who was usually the chief of the most powerful tribe. Passaconaway of the Penicooks, who lived near the present city of Concord, was such a leader among the New Hampshire tribes.

All the Indians along the Atlantic seaboard belonged to the great family known as the Algonquin. They were a brave, fearless, and dominant race who were greatly attached to their land, as, indeed, were all Indians. Directly west of New Hampshire, and closely bordering upon it, was the home of another great family called the Iroquois. They were even more enlightened than the Algonquin family. Their homes were larger, and they were bound together more closely as a nation.

Family Life. — All Indians were remarkable for their hospitality. No visitor was allowed to go away without partaking of their food. In fact an Indian would rather have gone without, himself, than to have had a guest neglected. Hospitality was to them an unwritten law that must be obeyed, and had become a part of the Indian nature.

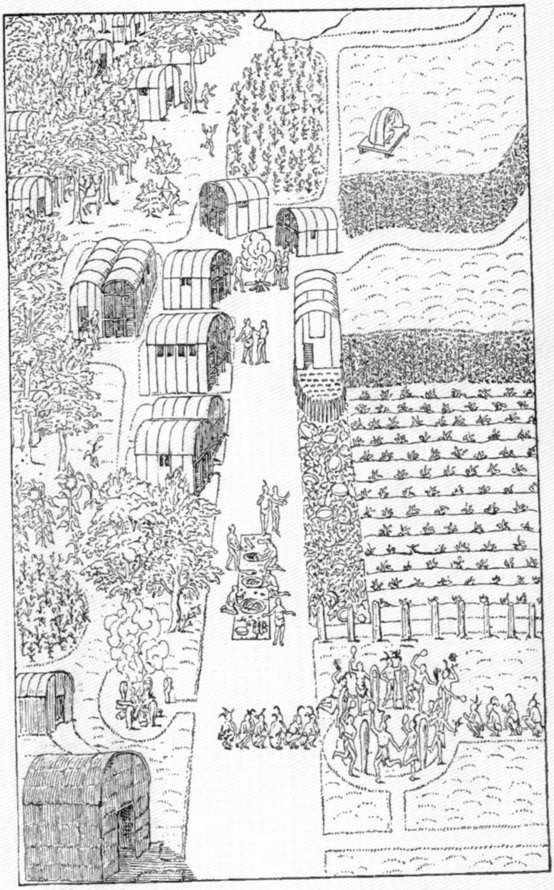

Plan of an Algonquin Village.
(From an old print.)

The villages, or small tribes, practically held everything in common like a large family, and what affected one affected all. The houses of the Indians when the first settlers came, contrary to the usual belief, were sometimes sixty or eighty feet long with a round roof, which was generally covered with movable matting, and in each house lived from three to twenty families.

Position of the Indian Women. — While, in a general sense, the warrior was the head of the household, yet within the home the mother was supreme, and the mother-right, as it was called, was very carefully guarded. The warrior, when he married, always joined the tribe to which his wife belonged. The wife, if the husband did not provide for the household properly, had the power to drive him away. The husband was looked upon as a hero, the defender of the family, the hunter, and the provider of meat. It is natural that, looking upon the man in this way, the woman believed it her duty to relieve him of all drudgery at home. For this reason we find the squaw doing all the work, planting and hoeing the garden, bringing the water and wood, not because she was driven to it, as many have supposed, but because she was willing to do the menial labor so long as the husband maintained his dignity as a warrior; but should he prove lacking in courage, no squaw would work for him.

In looking upon the man as a defender and a protector, the trust of the woman was seldom misplaced. It is said that an Indian once walked forty miles in order to obtain a few cranberries for his sick wife.

Another father cheerfully surrendered himself to be tortured, in place of his young son, who had been captured by an unfriendly band of Indians. This substitution was accepted and the boy was allowed to go free, while the father was burned at the stake.

Indian Hunters. — As hunters, the Indians were unsurpassed. Their only weapons were the bow and arrow, spear, club, and tomahawk, with which they killed the bear, deer, moose, beaver, wild pigeon, and other game. The secrets of the forest were an open book to them. They could track their game for miles through dense woods and over rocky ledges, where to the unpracticed eye there was no sign that any animal had passed. They were trained to be so watchful and observant, that a broken twig or a bent blade of grass told them not only that game had been by, but even what kind it was. When hunting, they often ran for hours without food or water with the most marvelous powers of endurance.

Indian Children. — Until a child was two years old, it was kept in a bag made of soft padded leather and usually slung over its mother's back, but afterwards it was allowed to run about and play with the other children. The boys were early taught to run, jump, swim, and wrestle, and the skill of even the small boys with the bow and arrow was very great. The older men took the keenest delight in teaching sports and games to the little ones, and they watched their improvement closely from day to day. Before the boy could become a warrior he had to pass through many trials of fasting. When fifteen years old, a fast of five days was imposed as a final test. While the boys were taught the arts of warfare, the girls were given lessons in hard work. They brought wood for the fire, and water for cooking, and were prepared thoroughly for their share of responsibility.

Boys were never whipped by their parents, who believed this punishment to be degrading, and acts of disobedience or insubordination were allowed to pass without the "thrashing" which our forefathers thought so necessary.

Many things were taught the Indian youths and instilled into their natures which would form an excellent foundation for manhood and womanhood in any people. Among them were hospitality, respect for the aged, truthfulness, honesty, independence, and courtesy. With these attributes, however, were taught the most remorseless desire for revenge and relentless cruelty toward enemies.

The boys and young men were very fond of games and were always good-natured, no matter who was victorious. They played shinney, football, tag, hide-and-seek, and a game which formed the beginning of our national baseball. The girls enjoyed their dolls and mud pies when not helping their mothers.

How the Indians Farmed. — All along the banks of the Merrimac and Connecticut rivers, in the rich, alluvial soil, the Indians had their small patches of cultivated land, in which the squaws planted corn, pumpkins, squashes, melons, and beans. In the spring, when the alewives came up the rivers from the sea, they were caught in great numbers and used to fertilize the hills of corn; for digging up the weeds they had a primitive kind of hoe formed from a piece of slate to which was fastened a handle made of strong withes bound with rawhide. In this crude way they tilled the soil.

Food of the Indians. — When the corn was large enough, it was cut green from the cob and boiled, and was known to the Indians as samp. When corn and beans were cooked together, the dish was called succotash. Hominy was made by pounding dry corn in a mortar with a stone pestle until it was made into coarse meal, which was then boiled. Baked beans, the dish which is typical of New England, came originally from the Indians. They made corn cake, baking it on flat rocks before the fire, and also gave to our boys and girls popcorn, which they called "the corn that flowers." It is said that the Indians were the first to make use of gruel for the sick room.

In the summer the women and children picked wild raspberries, blueberries, strawberries, and blackberries; in the autumn they went nutting for chestnuts, hickory nuts, and beech nuts, which they, like the squirrels, stored up for winter use.

The food was boiled in an earthen pot, which was made by lining a wicker basket with clay and sand. This was put upon the fire, and when the basket was burned away, a serviceable pot was left. Pieces of the pottery are found even now with the print of the basket work on them. Their spoons and ladles were made from seashells and their knives from flint.

Mechanical Skill of the Indians. — The Indians were by no means an unskilled race of savages. They had many mechanical contrivances of a high order, and their skill in handling rude tools was very remarkable. Their bows and arrows, usually made from the tough and springy hickory wood, were beautifully formed and exceedingly accurate. They also had spears for fishing which were like their arrows, only larger and longer, with a triangular piece of flint for the head. The war club was cut from a stout oaken stick with a heavy knob on one end, in which they often fastened jagged pieces of flint. Stone hatchets, or axes, were made in an interesting way. The head was carefully formed with a groove around it, and was inserted in a small, growing sapling which had been split for the purpose. It was allowed to remain in this position until the young tree had grown around the stone so as to hold it very securely, when it was cut off above and below, leaving a sufficient handle. Thus a very strong and durable weapon was made.

The squaws were skillful in tanning skins so that the leather was soft and pliable. From the tanned hides of the moose, deer, beaver, and other animals they made their moccasins and the clothing which they used in winter. For sewing, they used an awl-like needle made either from the bone of a fish or from a small bone taken from the leg of a heron.

In moving from place to place, the Indians often followed the rivers, and used the birch-bark canoe, or dugout, for this purpose. During the winter, when deep snows covered the ground, they bound snowshoes to their moccasins, and could travel as easily as in summer. The snowshoes were made of a light framework of ash, which was filled with meshes of rawhide, thus presenting a broad surface to the light snow. Besides spearing fish, they caught them with fishhooks made of bone and also with nets woven from the fibrous bark of the elm tree. They were skillful in constructing baskets, and sometimes made fish traps of basket work, very similar to the lobster pots common at the seashore. The fish could swim into this trap, but found difficulty in getting out.

Method of Making Fire. — The Indians produced fire in the following manner; — they first took a dry stick about a foot long and an inch in diameter, and after flattening both sides, so that it was about a fourth of an inch thick, they carefully made a small depression on one of the flat sides, a quarter of an inch from the edge. Opposite this hole a nick was cut in the edge, and was connected with the depression by a small groove. When these preparations were completed, the stick was placed on the ground and firmly held by the knees. Then a slender stick of soft wood, about the thickness of a pencil and from twelve to fourteen inches long, was rapidly twirled back and forth between the open palms in the small depression. In a short time a fine dust was formed at the junction of the two sticks and, passing through the groove, fell in a little heap within the nick mentioned above. Soon the heat caused by the friction set fire to the dust, which was carefully yet quickly transmitted to such inflammable substances as might be near at hand. By this method they were able to produce fire in from one to three minutes.

After the coming of the white men, the Indian became very improvident. The labor-saving devices which the English brought over, and which the Indians easily bought for skins, removed the necessity of working hard with flint tools in order to make the bow and arrow, the stone hatchet, and the kettle of clay.

Indian Cunning. — An incident which occurred at Plymouth, New Hampshire, shows the cunning and forethought of the Indian. Captain Baker, with a small band of men from Northampton, Massachusetts, had attacked and destroyed an Indian village at Plymouth. The Indians, however, were very numerous, and Baker retreated down the Connecticut as rapidly as possible, thinking that he would surely be followed and attacked. At the first halting place, where they prepared their supper, a friendly Indian, who was with the party, suggested to Baker that each man should build many fires and cut many sharpened sticks upon which to broil their meat. By this means the Indians, seeing a great many fires and sticks, would be deceived as to their numbers and would, perhaps, stop their pursuit. This idea was acted upon, and the pursuing Indians, coming upon so many camp fires, believed the whites too strong to be attacked and turned back, leaving Baker and his men to go to their homes unmolested.

The different tribes often fought with each other, and in these quarrels they used the same stealthy methods of attack which they were accustomed to employ in hunting wild animals. They have sometimes been called cowardly on account of their manner of fighting, when they were merely following their custom of being as economical of their lives as possible. If they were beaten they never asked for quarter, and if they were captured they expected to be tortured by their enemies, and gloried in being able to bear the most cruel suffering without complaint. While they were being slowly killed, they cften taunted their captors with a lack of skill in torturing them.

The Indian's Idea of Land. — The Indian could form no idea of the individual ownership of land. He believed that, like the sea and air, it had been given for the use of all men, and he could not see how a man was able to really own any of the earth. To be sure, they had their tribal limits beyond which they could not hunt or fish, but the right to hunt belonged to the tribe as a whole and not to any individual. For this reason, they parted readily with their land to the white settlers for a small sum, but they did not think that by so doing they were actually selling the soil. This misunderstanding was the cause of trouble and bloodshed. If the whites had taken more pains to learn the habits of the Indians, much of the suffering from the Indian wars might have been avoided. Among the few men who made a careful study of the Indian character was Eleazer Wheelock, the founder of Moor's Indian School, which later became Dartmouth College. His efforts to Christianize and to help the Indian, and his marked success, afford a shining example of what might have been accomplished with the New Hampshire Indians.

Little remains of the Red Men at the present time except a few flint arrowheads, fragments of their pottery, the Indian names of rivers, mountains, and towns, and here and there an old headstone in the corner of some forgotten cemetery, on which is inscribed, " Killed by the Indians."

CHAPTER III.

CUSTOMS OF THE SETTLERS.

Log Houses. — The houses of the early settlers, with their rough log walls and huge open fireplaces, make an interesting picture around which to group the more detailed life of this time. These log cabins were rectangular structures with openings cut through for windows and doors. The well-trodden earth served as a floor, and the roof was of saplings covered with birch-bark. The chinks between the logs were packed with moss and clay, so that not even the coldest wind could beat through them. Above the main room was a garret made by laying a floor of poles on a level with the eaves. Here was the children's bedroom, and often on a winter's night the snow sifted through the cracks of the roof and covered them as they slept.

A most important part of each cabin was its huge chimney, made of rough stones laid in clay. It is said that in those days the lightest part of the house was near the fireplace, for the chimney made such a large opening to the sky. Often the sides, projecting into the house, were made so roughly that they were used by the children as a staircase on which to clamber up into the loft.

The Open Fire. — The enormous fireplace consumed great quantities of wood, and it was no small matter to keep it supplied. To attend to the "working up" and bringing in of the day's wood was the business of the boys. Sometimes, when they had an unusually large "back log," they would fasten themselves to it by means of a harness, and, with a shout, all hands hauling together, the log, often six feet long, went bounding across the yard, through the door, and up to the fireplace, where it was rolled to the back, against the stones. Upon it was placed a smaller back stick, and in front rested the fore stick. When these were in position, the smaller wood was heaped upon the andirons before them.

In starting the fire, a piece of steel was struck sharply against a bit of flint, and the sparks which were given off were caught upon tinder, — a piece of charred cloth. The spark was then carefully nursed into a flame by gently blowing upon it. In later years small sticks with both ends dipped in sulphur were used to assist in making a fire. When once lighted, it was supposed never to go out. During the night the father tried to "keep fire" by burying a hard wood brand in the ashes. If for any reason no live coals could be found in the morning, the boys were sent to the nearest neighbor to "borrow fire."

In case there were no neighbors, the laborious process with the flint and steel had to be repeated. When it was fully started, a glorious blaze was the result. In the evening each crack and corner of the cabin was well lighted, and no more cheerful scene can be imagined than the family circle gathered about the fireplace, the grandfather seated in the high-backed settle, and the children in the chimney corner.

Over the coals the women of the family did their cooking. The pots and kettles were suspended by a chain and hook, which hung from a wooden bar, placed across the chimney and high enough to be free from the danger of burning. Later, an iron crane was fastened on hinges at the side of the fireplace, by which the goodwife could more easily swing her pots and kettles on and off the blaze.

Methods of Cooking. — The Dutch oven was the earliest form of a baking utensil. It was a shallow iron pan with a tightly fitting cover. When the bread had been placed within, it was put in the hot ashes and covered with glowing coals. The more common method of baking was by means of stone ovens, made in the chimney at the side of the fireplace. On baking day, which was generally once a week, the oven was filled with hot coals, and after the sides had become thoroughly heated, they were raked out and the brown bread, beans, pies, and puddings were placed within. A door, usually of wood, was then set at the mouth of the oven and kept there until the food was cooked.

The meats were always roasted before the open fire, either upon a spit, a long iron rod with a crank at one end, which rested on hooks placed in the andirons, or by means of a hook and line. With the latter the meat was suspended before the fire, and by turning the piece round and round, the string was tightly twisted, and when left alone would slowly unwind, thus exposing every side of the meat to the heat. To see that this winding process continued, a small boy was chosen and was armed with a long stick to keep up the motion. Besides roast venison, bear meat, turkey, and other game, our forefathers' food consisted of beans, peas, squashes, pumpkins, and turnips. The cooking was of the simplest character, but their out-of-door life gave them excellent appetites, and an abundance was always provided. They were very hospitable people, and the stranger, as well as the neighbor, was always made welcome to a share in the dinner or supper, as the case might be.

Coarsely ground Indian meal served as a basis for many dishes, and hominy formed a staple article for the evening meal. The early settlers were very fond of the dish called bean porridge. It was made by boiling beans with the liquor in which corned beef had been cooked. They believed that the longer the bean porridge was kept, the better it became.

Oftentimes the goodman of the household, when compelled to make a journey in the winter, would be provided with a frozen cake of porridge, and from this, as hunger overtook him, he would break off and thaw out pieces for his luncheon.

The method of cooking pumpkins was peculiar. Having selected one which was thoroughly ripe, a small hole was cut in the top and the seeds were removed; after it had been well baked in the oven, the soft pulp on the inside was eaten with milk and considered a great delicacy. The outside shell, hardened by baking, was often used by the grandmother for a workbasket.

Bread was made of rye and Indian meal mixed, and resembled the brown bread of to-day. Our wheat bread was then unknown.

Cooking Utensils. — The women took especial pride in keeping all of the copper and pewter cooking utensils scoured to a most remarkable brilliancy, especially the plates, platters, and porringers, which they kept for show on a set of shelves called a dresser. The everyday plates, made of wood, were usually square in shape, but it was no uncommon thing for the family to dispense with plates entirely, and to gather around and eat from the same kettle. Forks were unknown, and next to spoons, fingers were most often used. Spoons, like plates and ladles, were made from pewter, which is so soft that they had to be very thick and clumsy and were even then easily broken.

Traveling Workmen.—Men used to travel from house to house with ladle and spoon moulds. They would melt up the broken and worn-out spoons and run them into moulds. When cool, the articles were as good as new. The shoemaker, in like manner, traveled from one family to another. With his hammer and waxed ends he made the outfit of boots for the entire household, the leather being provided by the father from the tanned skins of his own cattle. For the purpose of making leather, many tanneries were scattered about on the banks of the small streams.

All clothing at this time was homespun, and it devolved upon the women of the household to card and spin the wool, which was then woven into cloth. In families where there were many children, the mother was often unable to provide more than one set of clothes apiece, and, as a result, when these needed washing, the children had to go to bed while it was done. The story is told of one economical goodwife that she made her boys wear their shirts part of the time with the back toward the front, so that there might be an equal wear on both sides.

The knee breeches of the men were sometimes made from the dressed skins of the deer or sheep and were exceedingly durable, but were apt in wet weather to stretch, and impede the progress of the person wearing them.

As may be judged, the women of these early days were compelled to be industrious. For a person to buy clothing was considered the height of extravagance. In every homestead were cards and a great wheel for spinning the woolen thread, also the little wheel with its reel and its swifts for the linen, while in every kitchen was placed the dye tub, in which the linen and the woolen cloth were colored.

Process of Making Linen Cloth. — The Scotch-Irish were particularly skillful in raising flax and in weaving linen. Before they came to America, the linen cloth made in the colonies had been very coarse and rough, but they produced such fine goods that the linen of New Hampshire was famous throughout New England.

It is interesting to note the methods used by our ancestors in the manufacture of linen. After the flax was pulled and the seeds threshed out, it was placed out of doors and exposed to the weather, in order that the woody part of the flax might become tender enough to separate easily from the fibres. In the month of March, after the snow had left, the flax was gathered into barns, and the softened woody part was removed by a process which was called breaking. Afterwards, the flax was "swingled." This was done by pounding it with a heavy wooden knife which served to separate the fine fibres from the coarser tow. It was then combed, that is, it was drawn over a rough, iron-toothed comb again and again, which drew out all the imperfect fibres from the flax, when it was ready for the distaff and the spinning wheel.

Maple Sugar Making. — In the early spring, before the snow had gone, and just as the buds were begin-

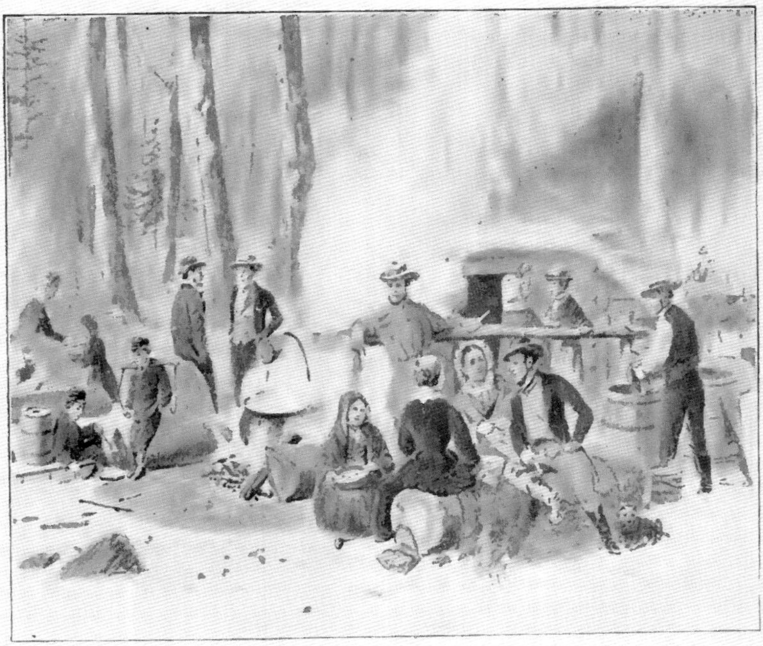

Maple Sugar Camp.

(From an old print.)

ning to swell on the maples, the men and boys would journey to the mountain sides, where rock maple trees were plentiful, and there make a sugar camp. They first went about from tree to tree, and, while one with a sharp axe cut through the bark, in which he put a chip for the sap to run out on, the other placed the wooden troughs beneath, in which the "sweet water" slowly accumulated. After it was gathered, the sap was placed in a huge kettle and suspended over the fire in such a way that it could be easily swung off the blaze when required. Made thus in the open air, the cinders and sparks fell into the syrup and rendered it rather dark colored, but, nevertheless, to the children maple sugar meant all that was good and sweet.

When almost boiled down to sugar, a little of the hot, thick syrup was taken from the kettle and spread on pans of snow; the "maple wax" thus formed made most delicious candy not only for the children, but for the older people as well. The Indians taught the settlers the uses of maple sugar, and it makes one other good thing which we have received from them.

Hunting and Trapping. — During the winter, when there was little work about the house, the older boys generally spent their time in hunting and trapping. The woods and streams abounded in fur-bearing animals, and their skins, being highly prized by ladies in England, were easily exchanged for powder, lead, tea, and other things which the settler could not produce. Steel traps were unknown, and they used the Indian device called figure four traps. The black bears, which were very troublesome through their fondness for corn, were caught in what were known as "dead falls." The trapper first felled a good-sized tree along the base of which a semicircle of stout stakes was driven into the ground. The butt of the tree was then raised and a figure four trap was put in the semicircle of stakes, baited with a piece of fresh meat. When the bear went in to eat the bait, the tree trunk fell, breaking his back.

Means of Exchange. — Money was very scarce, and men had to barter or exchange things of which they had an abundance for those which they needed. The Indians, with their flint tools, laboriously cut out from the curly part of shells, or from the dark spots in clam shells, beads an eighth of an inch through and a quarter of an inch long, which they called wampum. To the Indians they represented a great deal of painstaking work and were highly valued. There were two kinds, the white and the black, and one black bead was worth two white ones. The beads were strung on threads of buckskin, and the Indians adorned themselves with belts made from several of these strings bound together. The Dutch in New Amsterdam first thought of using wampum for money, and the idea spread until it was used all over New England.

Founding a Home. — It was often difficult for a young man with very little money to purchase land in the older settlements and to make a home for himself, so it became necessary for him to start out into the wilderness, where the land was unclaimed. Usually three or four men banded together, and with their axes, guns, and a little corn meal went into the pathless forest, "blazing" the trees along their way. When they came to a piece of land which they thought suitable for making a home, a rough cabin was built for a temporary shelter, and then each cleared the land set apart for himself. They were all skillful axe-men, these young settlers, for, in those days, all the firewood of the house was "got up" and split by the boys; the constant practice made their arms strong and their eyes true, so that, in what would seem a very short time, they could clear off the trees from enough ground for the support of their families.

In clearing the forest they did not, as one might suppose, chop every tree entirely off, but, having found a number of trees in a line, they partly chopped each one, and then felled a large tree on the end of the line and let it fall against the second to knock it down. The second brought down the third, the third the next one, and so on, until, with a noise and cracking like thunder, the entire line came crashing to the earth.

As there were no good roads to the harbor, the trees were worth nothing for lumber, so that every effort was made to get rid of them as fast as possible.

This was done by burning. The young men, after clearing sufficient land, would return to their homes and wait patiently until the hot summer sun should dry the sap in the felled trees, so that they could have a burn, as it was called. When the wind and the weather were favorable, they set fire to the fallen trees, and with a tremendous whirling and rushing sound the giants of the forest passed off in fire and smoke, leaving only their ashes behind. These ashes were of importance to the settlers, as they were exceedingly valuable for enriching the soil. Great crops of pumpkins and of corn could be raised from the little patches among the half-burned stumps and logs.

When the land was cleared, each of the young men made a cabin on his own share and then went back to the settlement and brought his wife to live with him in his new home. Often there was no road to their farms, and they had simply blazed trees to follow. The corn had to be carried to mill many miles over such rough paths, either on a man's back or on a horse.

Mills for Grinding Corn. — One of the first things that the settlers did was to construct grist mills for grinding corn and grain. They built the mill beside a swiftly running brook, for the falling water furnished the power to turn the wheel. The dam was built as it would be now, only more simply. Under the dam, where the water falls over, a huge wheel was placed with buckets on its rim. As the buckets filled at the top, the weight of the water carried the wheel around, which was made to turn two large flat stones, one upon the other. The corn, or grain, sifted down between these stones and was ground into meal. It took longer to grind the grain than it does now, and the meal was much coarser. The miller was paid for his labor by receiving a certain portion of the corn, or, perhaps, by the skins of the beaver or the otter which the settler had trapped during the winter.

Trials of Strength and Skill. — It was customary at the raising and moving of buildings, at town meetings, and at other gatherings where large bodies of men met together, to have trials of strength and skill. Lifting heavy weights, pitching quoits, throwing iron bars, pulling sticks, and wrestling were taken part in and enjoyed by every one. Wrestling, which might be termed the typical sport of our forefathers, was always sharply contested by the men and boys. Usually the boys started the contest, and each defeated party brought in his champion to meet the victor. Thus the match went on, until the boys' places were gradually taken by men. The one who threw his man in the last encounter was said to have "carried the ring." All men distinguished in wrestling were known not only by their own townspeople, but often their reputation spread through the neighboring villages. It was customary for these champions to travel many miles for a trial of skill.

The following anecdote from the "History of Manchester" is characteristic of the times. A person called at the house of John McNeil of Londonderry, having heard of his strength and skill as a wrestler. McNeil, however, was away from home. The stranger informed Mrs. McNeil that he regretted this exceedingly, as he had traveled a long distance for no other purpose than to "throw him."

"An' troth, mon," said Mrs. McNeil, "Johnnie is gone, but I 'm not the woman to see you disappointed. An' I think if ye 'll try, mon, I 'll throw ye meself."

The stranger, not liking to be made fun of by a woman, accepted the challenge, but no sooner had they taken hold when, by a deft "trip and twitch," the man's heels flew up, and his back was laid squarely on the ground. Upon arising, he decided not to wait for Johnnie, and, in fact, did not even leave his name.

Shipbuilding and Commerce. — One of the important resources which helped in developing our state was the great quantity of codfish off the coast. The colonists soon built boats from their lumber, and spent much time in fishing. The fish was dried, salted, and shipped to foreign countries, where it was in constant demand. Thus a profitable commerce grew very rapidly.

Shipbuilders soon came from England who taught the settlers how to build boats. They were usually two-masted vessels, called "ketches," and very few of them were over a hundred tons burden. Loaded with staves for making wine barrels, and with salt fish, they were sent to Barbadoes, in the West Indies, where the cargo was exchanged for cotton cloth, sugar, molasses, rum, indigo, salt, and sometimes negro slaves; often they went to Italy, Spain, or Portugal and brought back oil and wine.

Little coasting vessels, manned only by a "captain" and an apprentice boy, traded between Piscataqua (Portsmouth), Boston, Plymouth, and other New England towns, and even sailed as far as New Amsterdam and Virginia for tobacco. Each sailor on these trips usually owned a small portion of freight, the profit from which "venture" belonged to him, after he had paid a certain sum for the transportation; this practice helped to interest the men in the success of the voyage. Gradually the vessels were increased in size and number. At one time Portsmouth had over two hundred boats of two or three hundred tons burden.

While the colonists were paying so much attention to ocean traffic, they did not neglect their inland trade, but built roads between the settlements, bridged the streams, and established taverns at convenient distances. Travel along these roads was almost entirely on horseback.

Early Schools. — The New Hampshire people have always taken great pride in education. One of the first buildings put up in a town, after the meeting-house was completed, was a log schoolhouse. In 1647 a law was passed requiring that a school should be kept in every town of fifty householders. The teacher, usually a man, was given about fifty dollars a year for his services.

Along three sides of these first schoolrooms were placed slabs upon which the older pupils wrote and worked their sums. The slabs were fastened by one edge to the walls of the building, the other edge being supported by legs driven securely into auger holes in the floor. For seats, hewn planks were used into which stakes were driven. Inside of this outer circle were seats for the younger children. This arrangement made it necessary for the pupils to sit facing the walls with their backs toward the teacher. In the center of the room was placed the master's desk, and from his throne he watched with eagle eye the work of the youths under his charge. One may easily appreciate the feelings of the mischievous boys, who, with their backs toward the teacher, were never certain when he was not looking at them. This feeling of insecurity must have been heightened by the knowledge that there lay on the desk a hickory switch long enough to reach every boy in the room, and that, too, without the master leaving his chair.

On the third side of the schoolroom was the huge fireplace with large, flat stones for andirons. Inasmuch as the chimney was never very high, and as green wood was burned, oftentimes the first part of the morning exercises was conducted in a cloud of smoke. The building of the fire was allotted to the older boys, who took turns in attending to this duty, as well as to the splitting of the wood. The older girls kept the room swept and cleaned. The windows were placed high, so that the attention of the children should not be distracted by outside affairs.

To schools of this description our ancestors trudged. Fortunate were those who lived near. Many, however, were compelled to walk several miles after having helped their fathers with the chores, or their mothers with the household duties.

The Meeting-House and Pound. — Near the meeting-house was stationed the pound, a stone enclosure where stray cattle were kept and from which they could not be claimed until a small fine was paid by the owner. Often the sexton of the church was appointed pound-keeper in order that the fees of the one might supplement the pay of the other. The meeting-houses were usually large, barn-like structures and without the steeple so characteristic at the present time. The pews were high, square boxes, with cushionless seats, on which the small boys sat and squirmed during sermons seldom less than two hours long.

Directly in front of the high pulpit with its overhanging sounding-board was a broad bench known as the deacons' seat. The aged deacons were accustomed to protect their heads from drafts by wearing bright colored flannel caps; and sitting in full gaze of the congregation, they presented a most imposing and venerable appearance. It was their duty to "line the hymn" which they did by reading two lines of a stanza, after which the congregation joined them in singing the same. Then two more lines were read and sung in like manner, and this was continued to the end of the hymn.

Stoves were unknown in these old meeting-houses, and even in midwinter the congregation sat and shivered through the long sermons and prayers. However, an exception was made of the older women who brought small foot-stoves of perforated sheet-iron in which were placed pans of glowing coals. Often when they lived at a distance, they filled their pans at some of the neighboring houses.

Duties of the Tithing-Man.—An official whose duties would be considered strange at the present day was the tithing-man. It was his place to see that the Sabbath was respected by all people; that on that day there should be no work, travel or amusements of any kind, no loafing around the tavern or other unseemly conduct. On Sunday, while service was being held, he was provided with a "black staff ten feet in length, tipped at one end with brass or with pewter" and armed with this implement, he quietly touched a slumbering elder or punched a mischievous boy.

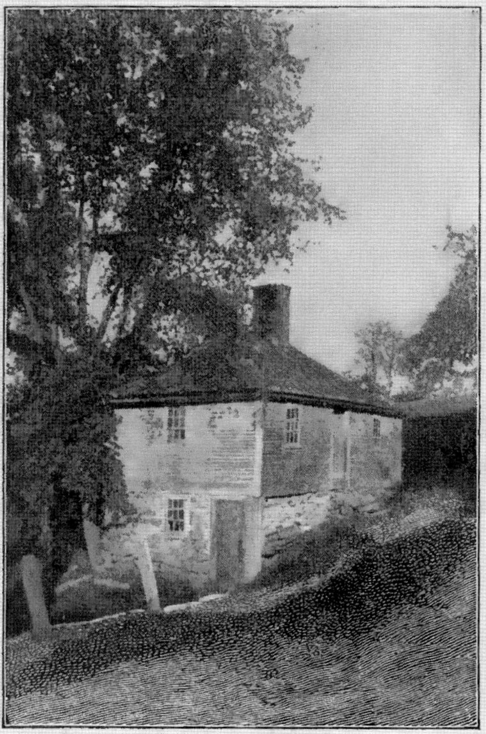

The Sullivan Slave House.

Everybody was supposed to attend meeting. The goodman and goodwife usually rode on horseback, the wife seated behind her husband on a "pillion," while the children trudged "across lots" on foot. An example of thrift may be learned from the fact that the boys and girls, during the summer months, always walked to church, barefooted, with their shoes and stockings under their arms. These were put on before entering the building, and were always carefully removed after the services were ended.

The Keeping of Slaves. — Several of the old New Hampshire families kept African or Indian slaves and many vessels were engaged in the slave trade. A cargo of rum and of iron bars was often shipped to Africa and exchanged for negroes, who were taken to Barbadoes and sold. The vessel returned laden with molasses to be made into rum with which to purchase more slaves. Some of the negroes were brought home and sold in the market like cattle; however, slaves were not kept to any great extent in New Hampshire.

Serving an Apprenticeship. — The tradesmen were organized into guilds, or unions, and had very strict rules about admitting a new member. If a boy wanted to learn the trade of a carpenter, blacksmith, ship-builder, or sailor, he had to be bound out as an apprentice to a master mechanic, sometimes for seven years. During this time he was virtually owned by his master and had to work hard in return for his teaching and for his board and clothes.

The King's Trees. — The white pine trees growing in New England were very valuable as masts for the navy, and it was largely on this account that Britain became so great a naval power. Every large pine tree was marked with the king's arrow to be used for masts in the royal fleet and a tree thirty-five inches through was worth five hundred dollars.

These mast trees were often over a hundred feet

high, and it was difficult to fell them without breaking or cracking. Smaller trees were cut and laid in the path which the large one was to take when it went over, in order to break the force of the blow. Then the branches were lopped off and about two hundred oxen were used to draw or "twitch" it to the river bank. It was very hard to get so many animals started together, and when the log finally began to move they were not allowed to stop; if an ox fell, he was cut loose and another was put in his place without stopping the team.

Piscataqua (Portsmouth) was the headquarters for this trade until 1727. In 1665 as many as seven or eight ships at a time were loading masts in the harbor, and when the trade was at its height, Piscataqua owned two hundred mast ships. They went so often and so regularly that the mail was sent by them.

The pine and fir trees also supplied material from which the colonists made the best of tar, pitch, turpentine and resin.

Improved Methods of Building. — All this trading made the colonists richer, and the enterprising men were able to build more comfortable houses than heretofore. They were built of bricks laid in clay, and with a coat of smoothed clay plastered on the inside of the walls. The outside was then covered with narrow boards called "clayboards," which word was afterwards changed to "clapboards." Later, a frame was made of heavy timbers covered on the outside with clapboards and plastered on the inside, much as houses are built now. The lime for the plastering was made by burning sea shells. The colonists were also able to have glass in their windows, as they

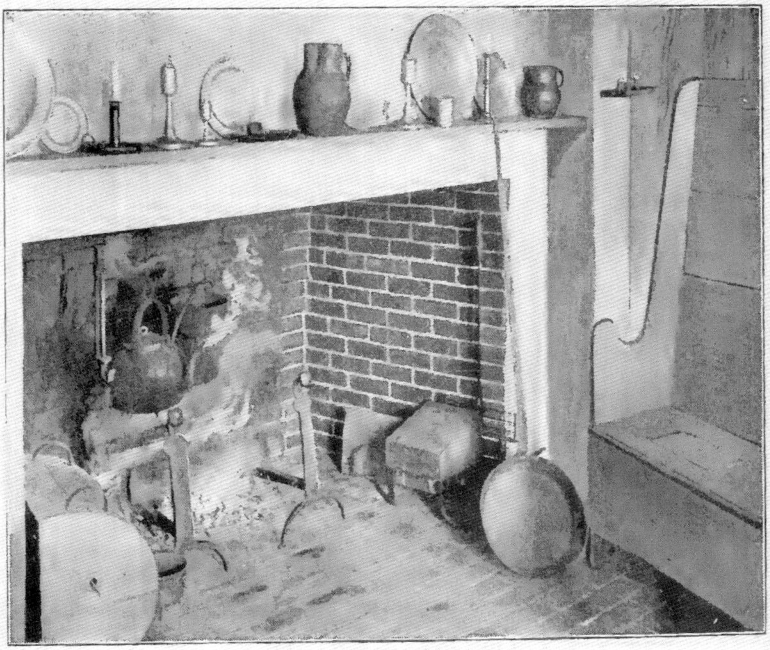

A Kitchen Fireplace.

could import it in exchange for their goods, or obtain it from Massachusetts, where there was a glass factory. The first glass was diamond shaped and each pane was very small and was set in lead, just as those of our stained glass windows are at the present time.

The first floor of the better class of houses had a large "keeping-room" or parlor, which was used only on great occasions. Then there was a kitchen, often twenty feet square, a bedroom, a cheese room and a butter room. A large brick chimney went up through the middle of the house with a great open fireplace in each of the main rooms and with closets in the space on either side. "The kitchens of the period were the true home centers and the best of New England life gathered around the chimney and the hearthstone."

As night drew on, and, from the crest
Of wooded knolls that ridged the west,
The sun, a snow-blown traveller, sank
From sight beneath the smothering bank,
We piled with care our nightly stack
Of wood against the chimney-back,—
The oaken log, green, huge and thick,
And on its top the stout backstick;
The knotty forestick laid apart,
And filled between with curious art
The ragged brush; then, hovering near,
We watched the first red blaze appear,
Heard the sharp crackle, caught the gleam
On whitewashed wall and sagging beam,
Until the old, rude-furnished room
Burst, flower-like, into rosy bloom:
While radiant with a mimic flame
Outside the sparkling drift became,
And through the bare-boughed lilac-tree
Our own warm hearth seemed blazing free.
The crane and pendent trammels showed,
The Turk's heads on the andirons glowed.

JOHN G. WHITTIER, "Snow-Bound."

CHAPTER IV.

POLITICAL HISTORY OF THE COLONY.

It is probable that the first settlements near the present sites of Portsmouth and Dover had a certain form of government as early as 1633, but the first written constitutions were adopted by the infant settlement in 1638 and 1639.

The officers of the Massachusetts Bay Colony were anxious to extend their possessions and inasmuch as their charter gave them the right to the land three miles north of the Merrimac River, they, with great ingenuity, sought to construe this clause as meaning three miles north of the source of the Merrimac, which would give them a goodly territory overlapping New Hampshire settlements and a part of Maine. With the end in view of supporting this claim, in 1631, Governor John Winthrop of Massachusetts sent Captain Thomas Wiggin to exercise control over the settlements on the Piscataqua. A collision naturally occurred between Captain Walter Neale, who represented the Piscataqua settlements, and Captain Wiggin. Neale dared Wiggin to step foot on a certain point of land half way between Dover and Exeter; while Wiggin proposed to defend his right by the sword. The quarrel terminated, however, without bloodshed, but in lieu of what might have been, this place was always known as Bloody Point and is called so to this day.

Despairing of obtaining a foothold by force, Wiggin, the next year, purchased the entire Hilton grant for about ten thousand dollars. As soon as he entered into possession of the Hilton patent, Wiggin endeavored to place it under the control of Massachusetts, but he was decidedly opposed in this endeavor by the original settlers, since they feared for the titles to their lands under Massachusetts jurisdiction. In 1640, when the settlers began to feel the need of the protection of a stronger state, and as Massachusetts promised them all the liberties which they had previously enjoyed, the opposition was overcome, and in 1641 the entire Piscataqua region passed into the control of Massachusetts.

It cannot be said that this union was perfectly satisfactory to the settlers of New Hampshire, and there was constant strife between the "Churchmen" of the settlements along the Piscataqua and the Puritans of Massachusetts Bay. Soon after the annexation, a number of the Puritans came to this section and by the aid of Massachusetts officials seized all the places of power and secured for themselves most of the unoccupied lands, causing the original planters to become more and more angry at their intrusion. As a result, two open rebellions occurred in attempting to withdraw from the union with Massachusetts, one in 1651, the other in 1664, but neither of them met with success. The union continued until 1679, when Massachusetts' control over Piscataqua was ended by the making of New Hampshire into a royal province.

New Hampshire a Royal Province. — The king appointed John Cutt president of the colony and instituted a council composed of prominent settlers of New Hampshire. Before this time Robert Mason had made such vigorous efforts to place before James II the Masonian claim to this territory that the king now appointed him to a seat in the New Hampshire Assembly. Shortly after, Mason, armed with a warrant and the king's favor, came to New Hampshire and tried to compel the settlers to purchase of him a lease for their lands.

In this, however, he was opposed by the president and the assembly. Finding his efforts unavailing with the present form of government, he returned to England, and, by promises, obtained the appointment of Edward Cranfield as commander-in-chief of New Hampshire. Cranfield was induced to take this office only upon Mason's guarantee that his salary should be paid.

Cranfield as Governor (1682). — Cranfield came from England with full power, and in a short time all officers of the state who were opposed to Mason were removed and others appointed in their stead. This, however, worked very little to either Mason's or Cranfield's advantage, for while they tried and condemned the settlers who would not take out leases of them, yet the force of public opinion was against them to such an extent, that they found it impossible to enforce the decrees of the court. The settlers continued to live on their lands, in spite of the officers and without taking leases from Mason.

Cranfield resorted to every expedient to raise money but was met with the most stubborn resistance by the colonists. Finally the people became so angry at his tyranny that they sent complaints to England which resulted in Cranfield's withdrawal in 1685. This left his lieutenant-governor, Barefoot, in control.

Barefoot's Trouble with Citizens. — Barefoot was not an improvement over his predecessor and used every means in his power to annoy the colonists. During his short stay an incident occurred which shows the contempt with which the government was held by the settlers. Thomas Wiggin and Anthony Nutter, who had formerly been members of the assembly, called one day at the house of Barefoot to remonstrate with him concerning the injustice of his proceedings. Mason, who was his guest at the time, was also present. During the discussion, the visitors told Mason very plainly and forcibly that his claim to the land amounted to nothing. This so enraged him that he took hold of Wiggin to force him from the house.

Wiggin, who was a powerful man, seized Mason by the collar and threw him with great violence across the room and into the fireplace, where his clothing and legs were severely burned. Barefoot upon coming to his assistance was treated even more severely. Several of his teeth were knocked out and two of his ribs were broken. Mason meantime called loudly upon his servants to bring his sword, but upon its being brought, Nutter quickly took it from him, and mocked the discomfiture of the highest officer of the state. Barefoot was followed by President Joseph Dudley, who in a few months was relieved of his command.

New Hampshire under Andros. — In 1686, the government of all New England was given to Andros, who won the reputation of being its greatest tyrant. All the power which he possessed was used to obtain money from the settlers. Upon the overthrow of King James of England, Andros was captured and sent to England as a prisoner of state.

New Hampshire without a Government. — For eleven months after the removal of Andros the colony remained without a government, when the settlers, realizing the need of a united force in meeting the attacks of the French and Indians, sent delegates from Dover, Exeter, Hampton and Portsmouth to draw up a constitution; but the town of Hampton refused to comply with its provisions and, as a result, it was without effect. Thereupon, the party which had always desired to be reannexed to Massachusetts, sent a petition to that colony asking for its aid and protection. The petition was granted and New Hampshire was restored to its former relations with Massachusetts.

Governor Allen. — This union remained until Samuel Allen, who had purchased Mason's claim, obtained from the king a commission as governor of New Hampshire in August, 1692. John Usher was appointed lieutenant-governor to look after Allen's interests during his absence.

The people distrusted Usher exceedingly, not only because he represented Allen's title, but because he had been a follower of the tyrant Andros. Usher was a merchant of Boston, a man of little education, but with a firm idea of his own importance. During his governorship there was a great deal of trouble with the Indians and he seems to have done everything in his power to help the settlers. They respected him for this and felt kindly toward him, but steadily resisted all his attempts to have them take out leases of their lands.

William Partridge, a well-known shipbuilder of Portsmouth, went to England and succeeded in being appointed lieutenant-governor in place of Usher. Partridge was particularly friendly toward the settlers, and during his short stay in the governor's chair the affairs of the colony were orderly and quiet.

Earl of Belmont — Joseph Dudley — Elseus Burgess — Samuel Shute — William Burnet. — The Earl of Belmont was next in charge of the state, and of the other British colonies. He was well received by the people and formed an excellent impression of the New Hampshire colony. Upon the Earl's death, Queen Anne appointed Joseph Dudley governor of both New Hampshire and Massachusetts. Elseus Burgess was appointed governor by George I, but did not come in person to administer the affairs of the colony during the year in which he held the office. He was followed by Samuel Shute, an able official, who was well assisted by his lieutenant, John Wentworth. The latter acted as governor during Shute's absence, and, through his diligence and thoughtfulness for the people's welfare, he became much respected. William Burnet acted as governor for one year, his administration terminating with his death in 1729.

Jonathan Belcher, Conflict with Massachusetts over Boundary. — Jonathan Belcher, who was the next governor, was a merchant of great wealth and of sterling character. During Belcher's administration, there was a long controversy between New Hampshire and Massachusetts in regard to the boundary line. While it was in dispute, a meeting was held between the legislatures of the two governments at Hampton Falls, with the hope that some agreement might be settled upon, but as is usual in such cases the parties were further apart at the close of the discussion than they were at the beginning. The question was finally decided in favor of New Hampshire, and several towns settled by Massachusetts people became a part of this state.

Benning Wentworth. — Benning Wentworth, son of John Wentworth, succeeded Belcher. He was well

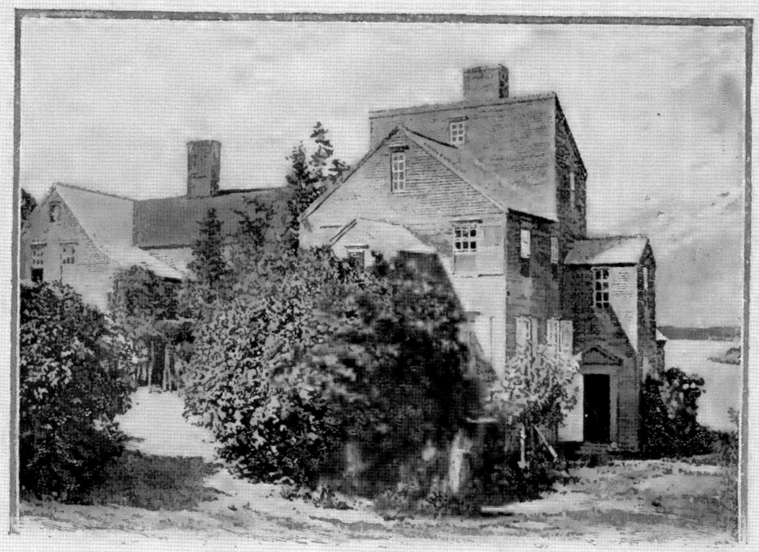

The Wentworth Mansion.

received, and voted a regular salary, and he obtained, by purchase, the office and title of Surveyor of the King's Woods. During the French and Indian War he took excellent care of his soldiers and received their hearty support.

Wentworth was very much of an aristocrat, and was fond of doing things in a royal manner. He boasted of the finest wine cellar in the colonies, had a bodyguard, and always traveled in state. After the death of his first wife, he desired to marry a young lady of Portsmouth, but much to his surprise and chagrin, she refused to become Lady Wentworth, preferring to marry a younger man. Wentworth, out of revenge for this slight, had her bridegroom seized by a pressgang and carried off to sea just before the time appointed for the marriage.

Afterwards the governor married a young girl beneath him in station. The way in which the wedding was brought about shows clearly his irascible temper. It occurred during a state dinner at the Wentworth mansion, at which many noted men were present, and among them a clergyman. When the guests were seated at the table, the governor introduced the future Lady Wentworth, and requested the clergyman to marry them. Upon his hesitating, Wentworth was much enraged and ordered him to perform the ceremony instantly. The frightened minister could only comply and he stammered out the marriage service. The misalliance was a great blow, not only to Wentworth's family, but also to the exclusive people of the colony.

Longfellow has made this incident of New Hampshire history the subject of one of his most graceful poems, — "Lady Wentworth."

He gave a splendid banquet, served on plate,
Such as became the Governor of the State,
Who represented England and the King,
And was magnificent in everything.

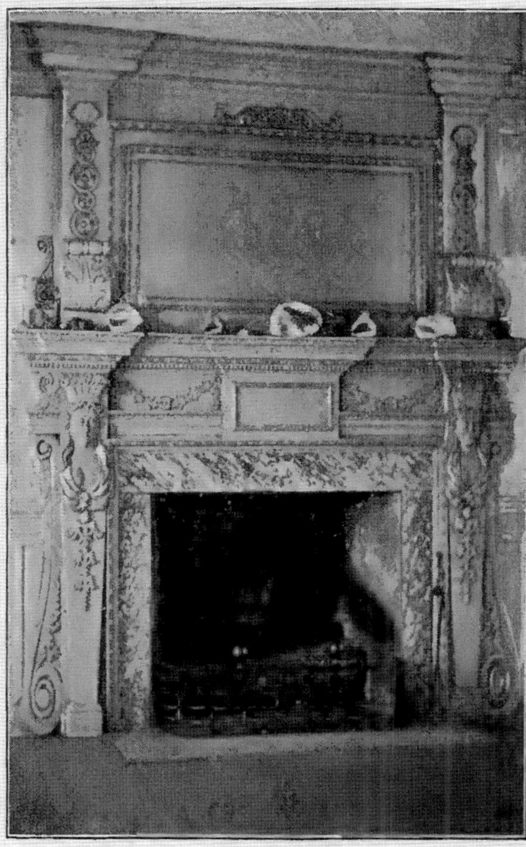

Fireplace in Wentworth Mansion.

He had invited all his friends and peers,—
The Pepperels, the Langdons, and the Lears,
The Sparhawks, the Penhallows, and the rest;
For why repeat the name of every guest?

But I must mention one in bands and gown,
The rector there, the Reverend Arthur Brown
Of the Established Church; with smiling face
He sat beside the Governor and said grace.

. . . .

When they had drunk the King, with many a cheer,
The Governor whispered in a servant's ear,
Who disappeared, and presently there stood
Within the room, in perfect womanhood,
A maiden, modest and yet self-possessed,
Youthful and beautiful, and simply dressed.
Can this be Martha Hilton?

. . . .

Yet scarce a guest perceived that she was there,
Until the Governor, rising from his chair,
Played slightly with his ruffles, then looked down,
And said unto the Reverend Arthur Brown:
"This is my birthday: it shall likewise be
My wedding-day; and you shall marry me!"

The listening guests were greatly mystified,
None more so than the rector, who replied:
"Marry you? Yes, that were a pleasant task,
Your Excellency; but to whom? I ask."
The Governor answered, "To this lady here;"
And beckoned Martha Hilton to draw near.
She came and stood, all blushes, at his side.
The rector paused. The impatient Governor cried:
"This is the lady; do you hesitate?
Then I command you as Chief Magistrate."
The rector read the service loud and clear:
"Dearly beloved, we are gathered here,"

And so on to the end. At his command
On the fourth finger of her fair left hand
The Governor placed the ring; and that was all:
Martha was Lady Wentworth of the Hall!

The governor's hasty temper and haughty ways of dealing with the people made him so unpopular that he was finally compelled to resign in favor of John Wentworth, his nephew.

Able Administration of John Wentworth (1767). — John Wentworth II, the last, as well as the most respected of New Hampshire's colonial governors, began in the best way possible to obtain the good-will of his people. He took a strong interest in all the common affairs of the province, was active in agriculture, surveyed the forests, laid out new roads, and stimulated activity and thrift among the people. He was a patron of the arts, and also of education. It was due to his efforts that Dartmouth College was begun with such favorable conditions, and under his jurisdiction the state was divided into counties, which was a great

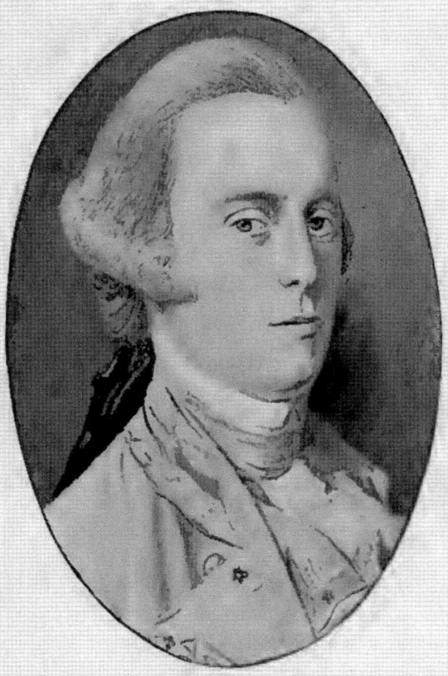

Governor John Wentworth.

convenience for those persons living in the western and northern parts of the state, since the county courts were able to settle disputes which formerly could be decided only by those at Portsmouth. The abolition of paper money was also a distinguishing mark of John Wentworth's administration. Silver and gold were gradually introduced and paper money was called in through the taxes, which placed the currency upon a solid basis, and obviated difficulties of trade.

Even after the battles of Lexington and Concord, Governor Wentworth seemed to believe that there was still hope of peace. At the general meeting of the council at Exeter, three members, favorable to England, were expelled from that body. One of them expressing himself too freely was assaulted by the enraged people, and he finally took refuge in the Wentworth mansion at Portsmouth. The people, aroused by the action, brought up a cannon and placed it in front of the house, at which they threatened to fire unless the man was surrendered to them. The governor, frightened at this demonstration, gave up the offender, who was taken to Exeter. As the king's representative, Wentworth felt so insulted by this action that he withdrew from the house and moved to the fort in the harbor. From here he went to Boston, to return but once again to New Hampshire, and then only for a day.

Forming of the Provincial Congress. — During the last part of Wentworth's administration, the assemblies, which were made up of delegates chosen by the people, had gradually withdrawn their support from the King. Their discontent reached its height in July, 1774, when there assembled in Exeter the first provincial congress. From this time to December, 1775, the people elected five congresses, and the fifth congress adopted a form of government which lasted throughout the war. In June, 1784, a new constitution was made which has remained practically unchanged to the present time.

During this formative period the name and influence of Meshech Weare of Hampton Falls was most prominent. He was a delegate to the five provincial congresses and for many years was president of the council and chairman of the committee of safety, which had charge of the affairs of the state when the council was not in session. Upon the adoption of the constitution he was unanimously elected the first governor of New Hampshire and held this office until his death in 1786. Meshech Weare was a man of sterling honesty and one who left his impress upon the form and character of the government.

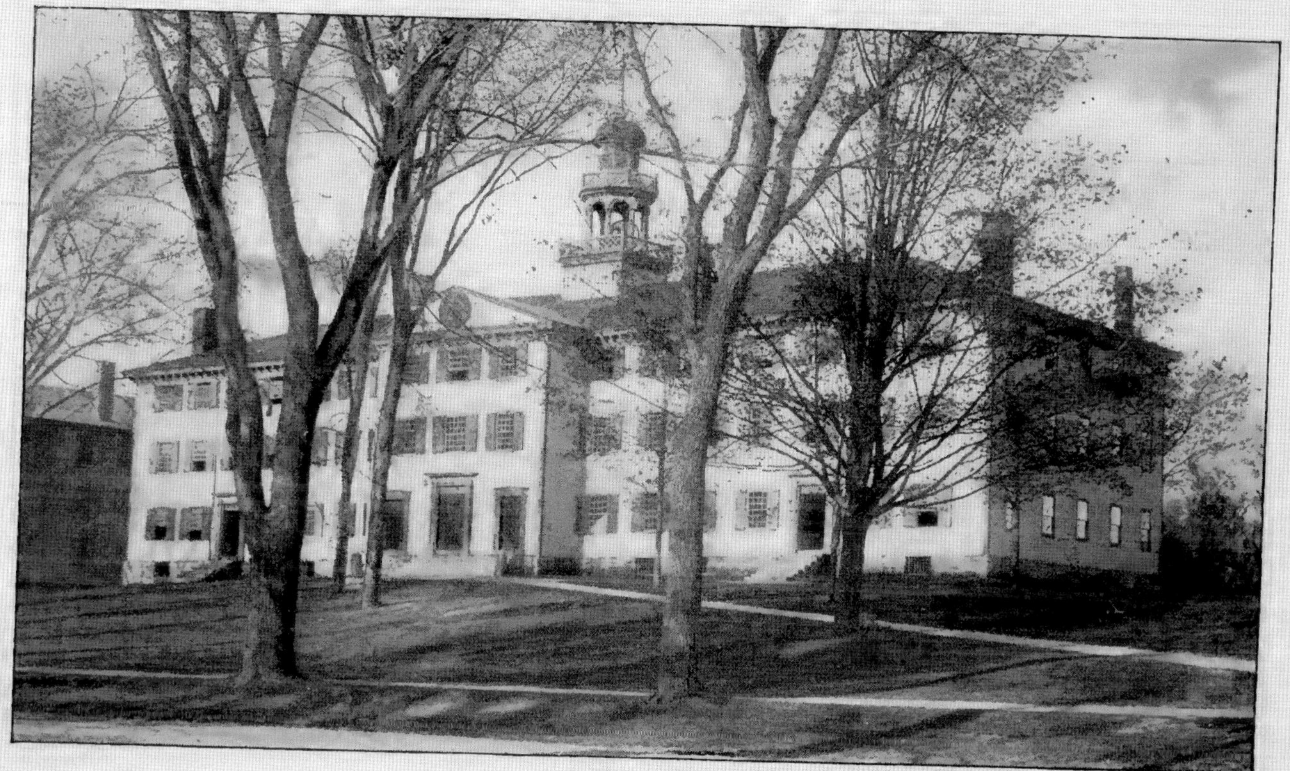

Dartmouth Hall.

CHAPTER V.

DARTMOUTH COLLEGE.

Dartmouth College had its beginning as a school for Indian youths, which was founded in 1755 at Lebanon, Connecticut, and was called "Moor's Indian Charity School" after its earliest patron, Colonel Joshua Moor, a wealthy farmer of Mansfield, Connecticut. For a time, only Indians were admitted as students, but later, English boys were taught with the understanding that upon graduation they were to become missionaries to the various Indian tribes. They met with such marked success that the numbers at the school steadily increased, so that in 1770 there were enrolled sixteen English boys and only three Indians.

Dr. Eleazer Wheelock was the founder of the Indian school, and it was due entirely to him that the institution enlarged its field and became Dartmouth College. In 1765 Dr. Wheelock sent to England one of his graduates named Occum, who was a full-blooded Indian, in order to show what might be accomplished in the education of the "Red Men." Occum's visit proved a remarkable success. He was received among the nobility and he created quite an excitement at London. He preached to immense congregations in England, Scotland and Ireland, and succeeded in raising funds to the amount of eleven thousand pounds for Wheelock's school in America, even King George giving two hundred pounds.

In 1770 Governor Wentworth, who for many years had been interested in the education of the Indians, voluntarily offered to Dr. Wheelock a large tract of land on the Connecticut River for the purpose of founding a college, and promised a most liberal charter for the institution. Wheelock accepted the proposition and went in person, in August of the same year, to superintend the work of preparing the buildings. The place selected for the college was a hundred feet above the level of the river and covered with an immense growth of pine trees, one of which, measured by Dr. McClure, was said to be two hundred seventy feet from base to top; in fact after the first six acres had been cleared, the surrounding forest was so high that the sun's rays did not strike into the clearing until late in the forenoon.

The workmen first built a temporary log cabin in which to live while the dormitory and the president's house were in process of construction. Before they were completed, the president's family with about thirty students arrived, having traveled over almost impassable roads and endured many hardships. What followed upon their arrival had best be told in Presi-

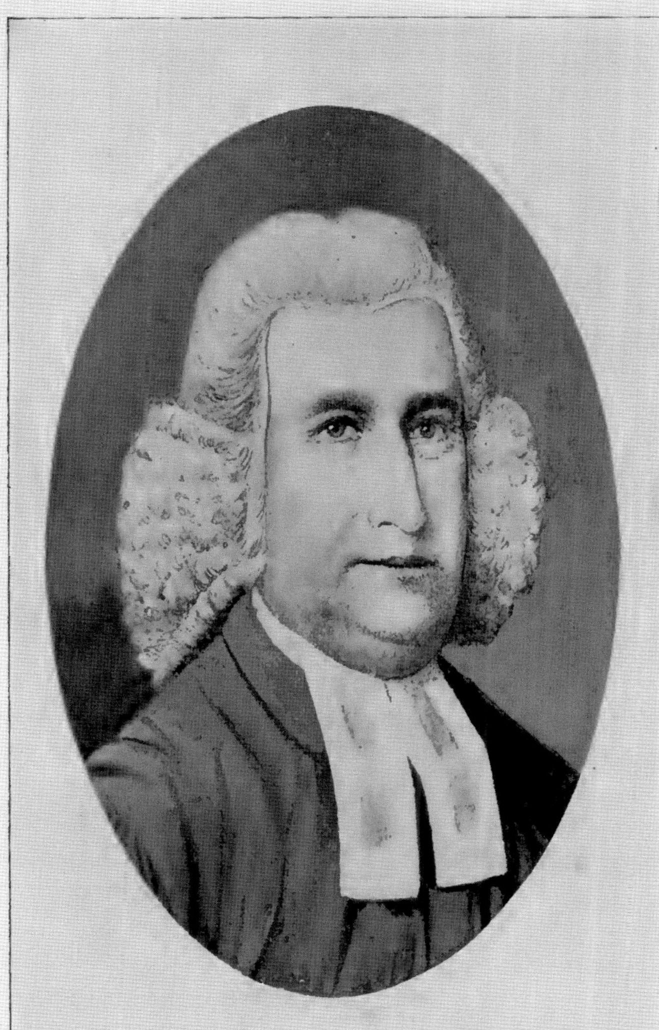

Eleazer Wheelock.

dent Wheelock's own words: "The message I sent to my family proved not seasonable to prevent their setting out, and they arrived with nearly thirty students. I housed my stuff with my wife and the females of my family in my hut. My sons and students made booths and beds of hemlock boughs, and in this situation we continued for about a month till the twenty-ninth day of October, when I removed with my family into my house, and though the season had been cold with storms of rain and snow, two sawmills failed on which I had chief dependence for boards, etc., and by series of other trying disappointments, yet by the pure mercy of God the same changed for the better in every respect, the weather continued favorable, new resources for the supply of boards were found till my house was made warm and comfortable, a schoolhouse built, and so many rooms in the college made quite comfortable as were sufficient for the students that were with me in which they find the pleasure of such solitude. And since the settlement of the affair, all, without exception, are sufficiently engaged in their studies."

Work upon the present Dartmouth Hall was begun in the summer of 1774, but it was not ready for use until 1791, as many difficulties in raising sufficient funds were encountered.

The first commencement was held August 28, 1771. Besides the trustees of the college, Governor

Wentworth and a number of gentlemen from Portsmouth were present. In order that the journey might be made in a manner suitable to the dignity of a royal governor, Wentworth caused a road to be made from Portsmouth to Hanover, a distance of over one hundred miles, extending for the most part through the unbroken wilderness.

The graduating class consisted of four students, and it is said that the exercises passed off in a very creditable manner.

From such small beginnings has the present Dartmouth College sprung. It ranks among the oldest of the American colleges, and it has established for itself a reputation of which every New Hampshire citizen may be justly proud.

CHAPTER VI.

TROUBLE BETWEEN NEW HAMPSHIRE AND NEW YORK.

The controversy between New Hampshire and New York over the lands of the present state of Vermont, then called "New Hampshire Grants," was long and bitter. The sovereigns of England, by whom large grants were made, had little or no conception of the vast extent of this country. The charters of the colonies of Massachusetts and Connecticut gave their possessions as extending westward to the Pacific Ocean, although at that time the Dutch had settled along the Hudson River; however, there was this condition:—"Provided that these lands have not already been settled by some other Christian power."

After the conquest of the Dutch possessions by the English, they were given by Charles II to his brother, the Duke of York, who was granted, according to the charter, "All lands extending from the west side of the Connecticut, to the east side of Delaware Bay," which overlapped the lands of Connecticut, Massachusetts and New Hampshire. The boundary between New York and Connecticut, and between New York and Massachusetts, was placed many miles west of the Connecticut River, because this territory had already been settled under grants from Connecticut and Massachusetts. The governor of New Hampshire took prompt measures to have his line extended in the same manner, but the governor of New York refused to acknowledge that any land west of the Connecticut belonged to New Hampshire; however, New Hampshire's governor still continued to make grants of land in the disputed territory, and the settlers bought and paid for them. It is said that he became enormously wealthy from fees obtained by these sales.

To stop the granting of land by Wentworth, the lieutenant-governor of New York sent forth a proclamation stating that New Hampshire had no power to make grants, and he printed the charter given to the Duke of York to justify his statements. Finally the controversy was brought to the notice of the king by representatives sent from New York. They presented to King George a forged petition purporting to be from the people who had settled in the disputed territory, declaring that they preferred to be under the authority of New York rather than that of New Hampshire. Acting upon this petition, the king placed the boundary between New York and New Hampshire at the Connecticut River. With great injustice the men in authority in New York claimed that this annulled any action taken before by New

Hampshire in regard to these lands, and that the settlers who had bought them from the crown under the authority of New Hampshire, would have to purchase them again under the authority of New York, although the king in 1767 declared that no grants whatsoever should be made by New York in the disputed territory.

Meeting for Organization. — Since the New York officers refused to recognize the titles held under grants from New Hampshire, the people determined to protect themselves, and for this purpose held a meeting at Bennington, Vermont, in order to devise means for the best way of resisting the efforts of those who would deprive them of their homesteads and lands. At this meeting they thoroughly organized a system of spying upon the New York deputies; no surveyor from that state could run his line, and no sheriff was able, however secret his approach, to make an arrest without resistance. Whenever a New York official became too zealous in performing his duty, the people had a playful method of capturing him and imprinting on his back with rods what they were accustomed to call "the beech seal."

Difficulties Encountered by New York Officers. — The New York sheriffs labored under a great disadvantage, in that the common people of their state sympathized more with the settlers of New Hampshire Grants than they did with their own authorities.

Sheriff Ten Eyck, being required to serve a writ upon a resident of Bennington and suspecting strong resistance, called out the militia to the number of seven hundred fifty to assist him in making the arrest. The settlers, hearing of this, assembled three hundred men to oppose him. About twenty of them posted themselves in the house of the offender, while the remainder divided themselves into two parties and took their station on either side of the road, behind ridges which happened to skirt the highway at this point.

The sheriff with his men marched unsuspectingly into the ambuscade and ordered the people of the house to surrender, threatening to break down the door unless his order was complied with instantly. "Attempt it and you are a dead man," came the reply. At this moment the ambuscading forces made themselves known, and displaying hats on the muzzles of their guns made a showing of twice their actual number. The rank and file of the "Yorkers" having no real relish for the business, and seeing the trap into which they had so nicely fallen, concluded that their presence was no longer needed, and without a shot being fired on either side, quietly withdrew, followed by the crestfallen leader.

The Green Mountain Boys. — Shortly after a military force was organized for the purpose of more effectually opposing the New York authorities, and the renowned Ethan Allen was chosen as leader. They took it upon themselves not only to discourage further activity on the part of the New York officials, but to rectify the mistakes which they had made in the past.

The proprietor of a sawmill at Otter Creek had been deprived of his property by a force of New Yorkers under Colonel Reid, who claimed that the New Hampshire title, purchased in 1761, was of no value, and placed in charge of the property a tenant of his own. Ethan Allen, hearing of this injustice, with a company of Green Mountain Boys turned out the New York people and reinstated the original proprietor. This action greatly incensed Governor Tryon of New York and Colonel Reid. The latter, with a company of his Scotchmen (the colonel had formerly been in command of the Forty-Second, or Royal Highland Regiment) marched to Otter Creek, and after forcibly ejecting the proprietor, left in his stead a rugged Scotchman with orders to hold possession at any cost.

The Green Mountain Boys being informed of this last move on the part of the Yorkers, mustered a force and in no gentle manner ejected the Scotchman with his goods. He, although forced to yield by superior numbers, still insisted in broad Scotch that "wie twonty guid broad-swoards I would hae defended my mill tho' ye had a hundred mon." The Green

Mountain Boys so admired his pluck that they offered him a large tract of land if he would join them, an offer, however, which he scornfully rejected.

Committees of Safety. — New York, finding that force did not serve her purpose, attempted to make friends with some of the prominent citizens by appointing them to office. To oppose this policy, committees of safety were assembled, who voted that no person was to be allowed to take any grant of land from New York, and that no one could hold office under her authority. For the violation of these enactments, the penalty was to rest with the decision of the court. The more common form of punishment was banishment from the colony, or the application of the renowned "beech seal," already alluded to.

Sometimes the punishment was more grotesque than harsh. In one instance, Dr. Adams of Arlington, who had openly sympathized with and aided the New York authorities, fell into the hands of the Green Mountain Boys. When brought before the court, he was sentenced to be hung for two hours in an armchair, beneath the sign of the famous Green Mountain Tavern, a hostelry noted as the starting place of many raids against the hated "Yorkers."

The towns along the Connecticut slope being more peacefully inclined had acquiesced to the rule of New York and had taken out new grants under its authority. They were subject, however, to so many indignities at the hands of the New York officials that the people in this section became thoroughly aroused. The trouble reached a climax when New York refused to adopt the Articles of the Association of the American Colonies. In the neighboring commonwealth where the articles had been accepted, no royal courts were permitted to hold session. The

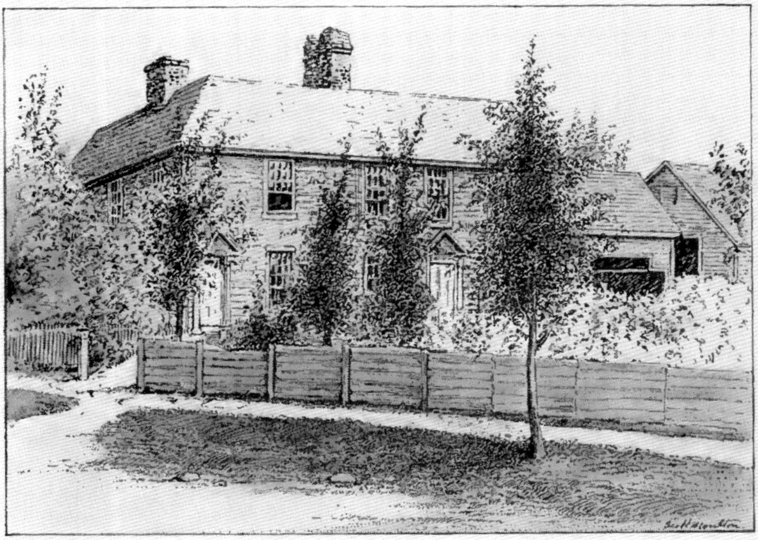

The Catamount or Green Mountain Tavern.

people being heartily in sympathy with this movement, demanded that no courts should be held there, although they were nominally under the jurisdiction of the magistrates of New York.

The Westminster Massacre (1775). — Upon learning that the authorities had determined to hold court at Westminster and had assembled a body of militia to enforce their action, a party of about one hundred settlers, in order to forestall them, seized the court-house the night before and determined not to leave until their claims had been heard. While here, they were fired upon by the militia under order from the sheriff. Two of the inmates were killed and several others severely wounded. The entire countryside was aroused by this action, and before the following morning more than four hundred men were on the spot ready to avenge the death of their neighbors. The sheriff and ringleaders were quickly seized and conducted to jail at Northampton, Massachusetts. The result of their trial was lost in the stirring times of the Revolution, but the outcome of the massacre was of great importance in preparing the way for the long struggle of independence that was to follow.

CHAPTER VII.

BEGINNINGS OF THE REVOLUTION.

The colonies were very heavily taxed to pay the expenses of the long French and Indian War. Taxes were imposed by the Parliament of England, and as the colonies had no voice in its decisions, they complained that taxation without representation was unjust. The English replied that many of their own cities had no representation in Parliament, yet they had to pay taxes; that the wars had been carried on for the benefit of the colonies, and that they ought to pay their share of the expenses. To this the colonists said that they were willing to pay their share, but the fact that certain Englishmen were not represented in Parliament did not affect the rights of the case.

In order to make the colonists buy sugar and molasses from her planters in the West Indies, England had passed, in 1733, what was called the Sugar Act, which placed such a heavy duty on sugar and molasses raised in countries not under her control, that none could be imported from them except secretly.

In 1750 Parliament passed laws forbidding the colonists to make iron bars. This act put a stop to the iron industry and closed shops in New Hampshire that had been rolling iron bars since 1747. They were called slitted iron and from them the blacksmiths and mechanics cut out bolts and nails.

Besides these unjust laws, Great Britain claimed the right to press New England sailors into service in her navy, whenever she had need of men. One captain was taken from his ship just as he was leaving the harbor of Portsmouth.

Pine Tree Law. — In 1710 all pine trees twelve inches or more in diameter had been marked with the "King's Arrow," which indicated that they were to be saved for use in the royal navy, and in 1722 the general court of New Hampshire had made it a criminal offense to cut down any of them. This law, as may be imagined, was very unpopular with the settlers, since they needed the lumber as much for building their houses as did the king for his navy. Governor Wentworth was appointed "Surveyor of the King's Woods," and had under his authority several deputies whose duty it was to see that the Pine Tree Law was properly enforced. To add insult to injury, if any man wished to clear his land, he must pay one of the deputies to come and mark the king's trees.

The Rioters at Weare (1772). — It happened at Weare, that a man named Mudgett fell under suspicion of cutting down the king's trees, and Governor Wentworth sent one of his deputies, named Whiting, to arrest him. The sheriff did not arrive at Weare until late in the afternoon, when he found Mudgett with several companions at a neighboring tavern. The prisoner protested against being taken away that evening, and finally prevailed upon the sheriff to remain at the tavern overnight, assuring him that his friends would be able to provide bail in the morning.

The townspeople, aroused and indignant at the arrest of their neighbor, assembled during the night and determined to show the authorities the contempt in which they held the "Pine Tree Law." A company of stalwart men was chosen, and at about four o'clock in the morning they rapped on the door of the sheriff's room and told him that the bailers of the prisoner stood ready outside. Whiting, grumbling at being aroused thus early, opened the door. He was then quickly seized, stretched over the bed and given his bail with good hickory switches which had been brought for the occasion. When sufficient bail had been administered, the much abused sheriff was taken down stairs, placed upon his horse, and amid the jeers of the people was led through the principal streets of the town.

These "rioters at Weare" were afterwards arraigned and each fined twenty shillings, which small fine leads us to think that the judge sympathized as much with the rioters as he did with the authorities. Of all the oppressive measures which the mother country imposed upon the colonies, none was so odious to the people of New Hampshire as the Pine Tree Law. It did more to unify our forefathers in active resistance against Great Britain than any other one thing.

Acts of Unjust Taxation. — The Navigation Acts, passed from 1650 onward, forbade the colonists to trade in any but English ships. These measures became so odious that it was impossible to enforce them, and smuggling was extensively carried on. In 1760, Parliament determined to put a stop to it and to enforce the laws. The sheriffs received orders to aid the collectors and were given power to search houses and vessels for goods that had been illegally imported. So strong was public opinion against this measure that the king's officers did not dare even to remain in the colony.

Nothing of English manufacture could be sold, and the colonists made every endeavor to supply necessary articles by home manufacture. This served as a stimulus to New Hampshire industries. A great impetus was given to the weaving of cloth in the homes, and one family, it is said, produced seven hundred yards in a year.

In February, 1765, the Stamp Act was passed, which enacted that legal papers and even newspapers must have a government stamp. They were sold by public officers, and the money was supposed to go for the protection and defense of the colonists.

When the ships bearing the stamps arrived at Portsmouth the bells tolled and the people assembled as for a funeral procession. A coffin with the word "LIBERTY" in capital letters engraved upon it, was borne to the cemetery on the shoulders of eight men, while the minute gun was fired. When they arrived at the burying ground, a funeral oration was pronounced and the coffin was lowered into the open grave. Then it was raised again with the inscription changed to "LIBERTY REVIVED," and with cheering and shouting the procession returned to the town.

In the English Parliament, Chatham and Burke upheld the conduct of the colonists, but Parliament would not recede from its position, and these oppressive measures continued to widen the breach between England and her colonies until war was finally declared.

CHAPTER VIII.

GENERAL JOHN STARK.

Early Life. — John Stark was born in Nutfield, now known as Londonderry, on the 28th of August, 1728. His father, a graduate of the University at Glasgow, emigrated to this country with several other Scotch Irish settlers from Londonderry, Ireland, in the early part of the eighteenth century. When John was but eight years old, the family moved to Derryfield, now Manchester.

In our backwoods settlements there was little or no opportunity to gain an education, and Stark's early life was spent in working hard upon the farm during the spring, summer and autumn, and in hunting and trapping during the winter.

He lived with his father until he was twenty-four years old, when, with his older brother and two companions he went on a hunting trip to Baker's River in the northwestern part of the state, beyond the farthest English settlements. While there, Stark having wandered some distance from the others, was seized by a party of ten Indians who demanded that he should lead them toward his camp. The young man had no idea of doing this, however, and con-

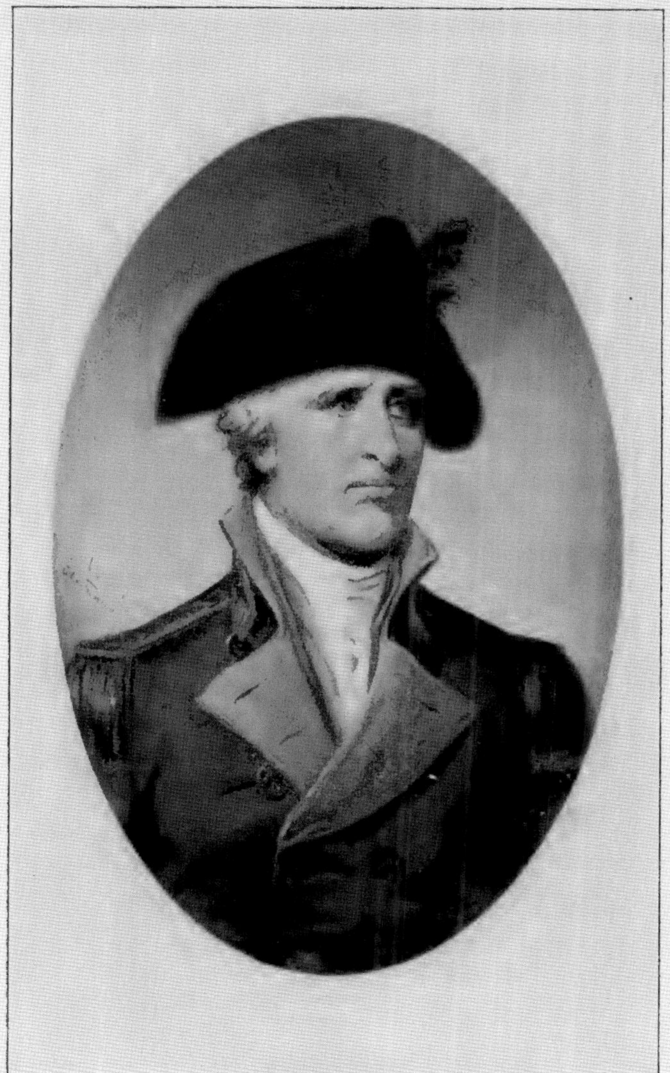

General John Stark.

ducted them in the opposite direction. But his companions, becoming alarmed at his long absence, fired guns and thus disclosed the true position of their camp. The Indians immediately turned about and made a stealthy advance upon them. As soon as they came within hailing distance, Stark, unmindful of the consequences to himself, shouted to his friends to make their escape. This his brother William was able to do, but of the two remaining, one was killed and the other captured.

The latter, with Stark, was taken to the Indian village of St. Francis where they were compelled to "run the gantlet," that is, they were forced to run between two long rows of Indians, each of whom, armed with a switch or club, beat the captives as they passed. Stark, much to their confusion, and to the amusement of the old men, seized the club of the first Indian, and used it with such effect that he escaped unharmed.

At another time young Stark was made to hoe corn with the squaws, but knowing that the Indians considered squaw's work degrading to a warrior, he carefully hoed up all the corn and left the weeds, to show them how ignorant he was of such labor. When reproved for this conduct, he threw the hoe far away from him and said, "It is the business, not of warriors, but of squaws, to hoe corn." The Indians were much pleased at his spirit, and adopted him into the tribe, giving him the name of "Young Chief." Although closely watched to prevent his escape, he had great liberty, and used all his opportunities for studying the character and habits of the Red Man.

Ransom of Stark. — When he had been with the Indians for some time, Captain Stevens of Number Four and Mr. Wheelwright of Boston went to St. Francis to ransom two citizens of Massachusetts whom they expected to find there. It had become the custom of Massachusetts to pay a ransom for her citizens who had been made captive by the Indians. Mr. Wheelwright advanced the ransom money, one hundred three dollars to Stark, and sixty dollars to his companion, when the two men returned to Derryfield after an absence of four months. Stark always remembered with pleasure this stay among the natives, and often said that he never saw any prisoner of war more kindly treated than he had been by them. New Hampshire refused to refund to Massachusetts the money for his ransom, and Stark went on another hunting trip the next winter in order that he might pay the debt himself.

Stark Made Lieutenant of New Hampshire Rangers. — The first Congress of the colonies, which assembled at Albany, New York, in 1754, planned several campaigns against the Indians, one of which, composed mostly of New England men, was to attack Crown Point on Lake Champlain. Robert Rogers enlisted a corps of rangers in New Hampshire to aid in this expedition, and Stark was made a second lieutenant in the regiment of Colonel Blanchard.

The army accomplished but little. They repulsed the French and Indians under Baron Dieskau, but did not follow up their advantage by attacking Crown Point. The rangers did such good work that Abercrombie, who had succeeded Governor Shirley, enlarged their numbers and Stark was advanced to the grade of first lieutenant.

Attack upon the French. — In the month of January, 1757, Rogers was ordered to take a part of his men on an exploring expedition from Fort William Henry. They started down Lake George on snowshoes, but some of the men became so lame that they were obliged to turn back. The remainder proceeded to Lake Champlain, where they captured a number of sleds loaded with provisions, which were on their way from Ticonderoga to Crown Point. From one of the prisoners they learned that there was a much larger force at Ticonderoga than they had supposed. Knowing that those who had escaped would inform the garrison of their presence, they began a retreat toward their camp of the previous night.

Advancing in Indian file, Major Rogers in the lead and Lieutenant Stark in the rear, they suddenly came on a force of two hundred fifty of the enemy, who immediately opened fire. Captain Spikeman was killed and several were wounded, but Stark and his men kept up such a steady fire that the rangers were enabled to form a line of battle on a hilltop, sheltered by trees. The enemy made an assault and the battle began in earnest. The contest lasted from two o'clock in the afternoon until dark. Rogers was wounded in the wrist, and one of his comrades cut off the Major's queue to stanch the wound.

Then the command devolved on Lieutenant Stark. When there was talk of falling back, he cried that he would shoot any man who retreated. In spite of the intense cold, the men having to stand in four or five feet of snow, the fight continued. A bullet broke the lock of Stark's gun. He promptly seized one from a fallen Frenchman. The enemy offered them every inducement to surrender, but they refused, and to such good purpose that nearly half the French force was mortally wounded. At dusk, the enemy stopped firing, and the rangers, knowing that they were very near a large garrison, resolved to retreat toward Fort William Henry. Assisting the wounded as best they could, they dragged themselves to Lake George, which was reached in the morning.

Although still forty miles from Fort William Henry, Stark with two other men volunteered to go there for a sled on which the wounded could be carried. Passing over the lake on snowshoes, they reached the fort about dark. Immediately they started on the return trip, and by traveling all night succeeded in bringing back the wounded at the close of the next day. It is said that Stark himself helped to drag the sled back to the fort, thus having labored for three days and two nights without stopping. In appreciation of his gallant conduct, he was advanced to the grade of captain in the place of Spikeman, who had been killed.

Stark Repulses an Attack upon Fort William Henry. — On the eve of St. Patrick's Day, Captain Stark overheard some of the soldiers at Fort William Henry talking of the way in which they were going to celebrate, and in order that his own men at least might be sober, he gave strict orders to the sutler not to furnish any liquor to the rangers except on an order signed by himself. When the men asked for orders, Stark complained that his wrist was lame and therefore he could not write. The French knowing that many of the garrison would be likely to drink hard on St. Patrick's Day, made an attack that night. As Stark expected, the regulars were unfit for service, and the fort would certainly have been taken had it not been for the New Hampshire rangers.

The Attack upon Fort Ticonderoga. — Both England and her colonies were determined to conquer Canada, and for this purpose large forces were raised in New England. New Hampshire furnished three thousand soldiers for the campaign of 1758. Loudoun was recalled and Abercrombie was put in command of the troops, which consisted of fifty thousand men, the largest army that had ever been seen in America. In July they marched against Ticonderoga. Stark, with his rangers, was ordered to go before and clear the woods of scouts and skirmishers.

Abercrombie delayed his advance so long that, when he finally made an attack, the French had received reinforcements and had entrenched themselves behind trees that were felled with their boughs and branches all pointing outward, making it almost impossible for an attacking party to charge through them. The English forces were repulsed with great loss, and although they still had twice as many men as the French, yet Abercrombie ordered a retreat. It now became the duty of the rangers to protect the rear as they had before protected the advance. No more work was done by the regular army that summer, but the rangers were employed in reconnoitering and in waylaying the baggage trains of the enemy. Stark, who was not needed, obtained a furlough, and returned to his home, where he married Elizabeth Page of Dunbarton.

After the capture of Louisburg, Sir Jeffrey Amherst was given command of all the Canadian forces. Stark, becoming tired of the slow way in which the campaign was conducted, soon resigned his commission and devoted himself to the care of his farm.

The Commencement of the Revolutionary War. — In 1774 Stark was a member of the committee of safety of his town, and he did all in his power to encourage his friends to stand firm for their rights and to resist oppression, even if it became necessary to rebel against the mother country. To this end, he greatly helped the militia in its organization and drill.

When the news came of the Battle of Lexington, the messenger, who was sent to ask Stark to take command of the New Hampshire forces, found him at work in his sawmill. He immediately stopped the mill, hurried to his house, took down his rifle, and started on horseback to Massachusetts, forgetting in his haste even to put on his coat. As he passed through the towns, he was joined by many other New Hampshire men eager to resist the British. Soon the New Hampshire troops were organized, and formed into three regiments commanded by Colonels Stark, Reed and Poor, with headquarters at Medford. Stark's regiment was probably the largest in the army as it consisted of thirteen companies.

Stark at Bunker Hill. — The night before the Battle of Bunker Hill, a party under Colonel Prescott was sent across Charlestown Neck to make a fortification. Two hundred of Stark's men were detailed to help in this work. The rampart which they raised was so unskillfully made that it was impossible for the defenders to fire, as the enemy advanced up the hill, without exposing themselves. Stark in derision called it a pound. Early in the morning, he sent two hundred men under Wyman, his lieutenant-colonel, to aid in the defense, and he, with Major McClary, went forward to view the situation.

It is said that General Gage, when he was reconnoitering the redoubt from Boston, was asked if the Americans would stand before the advance of the British regiments, and that he replied: "They will if one John Stark is among them, for he is a brave fellow and served under me at Lake George."

At two o'clock in the afternoon, Stark's whole regiment was ordered to the front and he hastened back to lead their advance. Each of his men was given a gill of powder, fifteen bullets and one flint; but their guns were of different sizes, and many of the men had to pound the bullets into the right shape for their barrels. They marched across Charlestown Neck, where they were exposed to a heavy fire from the British ships. Captain Dearborn, afterwards major-general, who was near Stark, suggested that they move faster.

"Dearborn," Stark replied, "one fresh man in action is worth ten fatigued," and he continued to advance in the same cool way. Stark was joined soon after by the two hundred men who, the night before, had helped raise the fortification. The men under Wyman were by themselves on the right wing commanded by General Putnam. Stark took his position on the left, between the fortification and the Mystic River.

The British forces, commanded by General Howe and General Piggott, landed under the protection of a tremendous fire from the British ships and from the artillery on Copp's Hill. Stark, seeing the engagement to be imminent, made a short speech to his men and ordered them to march quickly to a rail fence extending to the Mystic. There they gathered up the grass that had recently been mowed and raked into windrows, and placed it behind the fence. This, while no protection from the bullets of the enemy, served to deceive them.

Stark coolly advanced about thirty paces in front of his line, and carefully drove a stake into the ground. He then said, "If any man dares fire before the red-coats reach this stake, I will knock him down." The terrible work accomplished by the men behind the rail fence is well known. Twice the British forces retreated under the tremendous fire of the back-woodsmen, and it required all of Stark's authority to keep his men from following.

During the battle, word was brought to Stark that his oldest son, a lad of sixteen years, had been killed. The brave colonel replied: "This is not a moment to talk of private affairs when the enemy is in front," and he ordered the messenger back to his station.

Fortunately, it was a false report, for the lad was not killed, but lived to serve throughout the war.

Shortly afterward the fortification having fallen into the hands of the British, Stark ordered a retreat. All ammunition was gone and the Americans would have been at the mercy of the enemy, had not a supply of powder arrived from New Hampshire just in time to prevent a rout. It was the powder that had been captured at Fort William and Mary and stored at Durham. It had been brought over the hills to Charlestown by old John Demeritt, in his ox-cart, from the little New Hampshire town sixty miles away. With this ammunition, Colonel Stark was enabled to cover the retreat of the flying troops who had occupied the redoubt, and the entire force passed over Charlestown Neck in safety.

Expedition against Canada. — A portion of Stark's men, under the command of Captain Dearborn, joined the expedition which Arnold led up the Kennebec against Canada, but Stark himself remained at Winter Hill until the evacuation of Boston, March, 1776, when, under orders from General Washington, he went to New York, where his troops were engaged in strengthening the defenses of that city.

In May Stark was ordered to proceed to Canada by way of Albany and to join the American army. This he succeeded in doing, but the Canadian expedition was a failure, and the Americans retreated to

Chimney Point, on Lake Champlain. Here Stark thought that it was best for the army to make a stand in defense of the neighboring settlers, but General Schuyler ordered a retreat to Ticonderoga. The day after they reached the fort, word was received of the signing of the Declaration of Independence, which caused great rejoicing among the men.

Stark's Advice to Washington. — After the disaster at New York, General Gates was ordered to send reinforcements to General Washington, and Stark's regiment was included in the detachment sent for that purpose. Stark became impatient at the lack of active fighting and said to Washington: "Your men have too long been accustomed to place their dependence for safety upon spades and pickaxes; if you expect to establish the independence of these States, you must teach them to place dependence upon their firearms and their courage." Washington replied: "This is what we have agreed upon. We are to march to-morrow upon Trenton; you are here to command the right wing of the advance guard and General Green the left." Stark replied that the position exactly suited him. The attack was a great success, for several cannon and a large number of small arms were captured, and nearly a thousand men were taken prisoners, while the American loss was about ten men.

Just before the battle of Princeton, the term expired for which his men had enlisted, but Colonel Stark, seeing that important work was soon to be done, succeeded in persuading them to reënlist for a period of six weeks. Such was their faith in their colonel that not one of them failed to respond, which is the more remarkable as the hopes of the American army were then at the lowest ebb, and men were constantly deserting.

Stark Returns to New Hampshire. — As this new enlistment was only for a short time, it became necessary for Stark to return to New Hampshire to recruit men for the campaign of 1777. By March, his regiment was full, and having reported that fact to the council of New Hampshire and to General Washington, he went to Exeter to await further orders.

While at home, Stark learned that a new list of promotions had been made out, and that his name had been omitted, while inferior officers had been set above him. He immediately notified the council and Generals Sullivan and Poor that he considered his treatment so unjust that he must surrender his commission. They tried to dissuade him but he replied: "An officer who will not stand for his own rights ought not to be trusted to stand for the rights of his country."

Although Stark considered that his dignity required his resignation from the army, he still took great interest in the cause and warned Sullivan and Poor of the defenseless condition of Fort Ticonderoga and of the northwestern frontier. At the same time he declared his willingness to return to the army when his country should need him. The council and house of delegates gave him a vote of thanks for his attachment to the cause of liberty. On his return home, he enlisted in the Continental army all the members of his family who were old enough to serve.

Burgoyne's Invasion. — In 1777 Burgoyne with a large number of American Tories, Indians, Canadians and Germans, started from Canada to join Howe at New York, and thus cut the Continental forces into two parts. The Americans had been easily driven out of Fort Ticonderoga, Washington had met with many and severe reverses, and the whole country was in a state of gloom and despondency. The Committee of Safety of the New Hampshire Grants applied to the legislature of New Hampshire for aid, but as the treasury was empty no assistance could be given. In this extremity, John Langdon, a Portsmouth merchant, and speaker of the assembly, thus addressed that body:

"I have three thousand dollars in hard money; I will pledge my plate for three thousand more; I have hogsheads of Tobago rum which shall be sold for the most it will bring. These are at the service of the state. If we succeed in defending our firesides and homes, I shall be remunerated; if we do not, the property will be of no value to me. Our old friend Stark, who so nobly maintained our honor at Bunker Hill, may be safely trusted with the conduct of the enterprise, and we will check the progress of Burgoyne."

Stark is Given Independent Command.— Langdon's generosity enabled the state to raise a force of men which Stark was asked to lead, but he refused to serve under any officers whom he had formerly commanded; and finally, rather than lose his services, the legislature gave him command of all the forces of New Hampshire, and agreed that he should be entirely independent of the national officers.

When Stark arrived at Manchester, Vermont, the advantage of this power was shown, for there he was met by General Lincoln, who ordered him to march to the west side of the Hudson. Much incensed, Stark asked: "By whose authority do you give this command?" Lincoln replied, "By the order of General Schuyler."

Stark thereupon asked Lincoln to tell General Schuyler that he (Stark) was able to command his own forces, and also gave to him copies of his independent commission and orders from New Hampshire. Schuyler brought this to the notice of Congress, which passed a resolution of censure upon the state of New Hampshire for giving authority without its permission.

Stark's purpose was to protect the New Hampshire Grants, and the only way of accomplishing his object was to remain on the east side of the Hudson and attempt to cut off Burgoyne's supplies from Canada, which plan afterward met with the hearty approval of Washington.

Battle of Bennington. — Burgoyne, believing that there were many Tories in the New Hampshire Grants, sent out a large detachment of Hessians, Tories and Indians under Colonel Baum to obtain provisions and possibly recruits. On the 14th of August, Stark received information that this force had arrived at Cambridge, about ten miles northwest of Bennington, and that they were intending to capture a large quantity of flour, stored at a mill near the town. He immediately marched his forces in that direction, and at nightfall met the enemy.

As the ground was unsuitable for an immediate attack, Stark withdrew his army about a mile and prepared for battle on the following day. The next morning he moved to attack the British, but it began to rain so heavily that he was forced to return to his camp. This delay unfortunately gave Baum time to throw up entrenchments in a strong position and to send to Burgoyne for aid.

On the morning of the 16th, the Americans were reinforced by the Berkshire militia, those from Pittsfield being led by their pastor, the Reverend Thomas

Allen. This gentleman advanced to the log cabin where Stark had his headquarters and addressed the General as follows:—"We, the people of Berkshire, have been frequently called upon to fight, but we have never been led against the enemy. We have now resolved, if you will not let us fight, never to turn out again."

General Stark asked, "Do you wish to march now, while it is dark and rainy?"

"No," was the answer.

"Then," continued Stark, "if the Lord should once more give us sunshine, and I do not give you fighting enough, I will never ask you to come again."

Shortly after the arrival of the Berkshire militia, Stark sent Nichols and Herrick with a detachment of five hundred men to form at the rear of Baum's entrenchment, and also sent to the right a flanking party of two hundred men.

The stolid German commander was entirely unsuspicious of these movements. He took no notice whatever of the little squads of farmers who passed by his camp dressed in their rough homespun, for, to his mind, no man could be a soldier unless clothed in uniform. He was destined later to change his opinion. The Indians, however, were not at all deceived, and held an entirely different view of the matter. They quietly deserted the British camp, complaining that the woods were full of Yankees.

The weather cleared up in the course of the day, and Stark advanced toward the fortification. Having placed his troops in position, about three o'clock in the afternoon he ordered an attack. Advancing in front of his troops and pointing to the enemy, he exclaimed, "See, men! There are the redcoats! We shall beat them to-day, or 'Molly' Stark will be a widow!"

For more than two hours the fight raged, as Stark afterwards said, "hotter than he had ever experienced." The New Hampshire troops advanced repeatedly within gunshot of the intrenchments and with accurate aim picked off the Hessian gunners.

At last Stark rallied all his forces and led a final charge upon the works of the enemy. Then followed a hand to hand encounter, in which both sides fought stubbornly and well. Stark's men were greatly handicapped by lack of bayonets, but in spite of it they, with their clubbed muskets, repeatedly drove back the charges of the British. Finally Baum fell mortally wounded, and shortly after his forces surrendered. The Hessian prisoners were treated civilly, but the Tories were fastened to a long rope two by two, the end of which was hitched to the tail of an old horse, and in disgrace they were marched through the town of Bennington.

While the Americans were still engaged in plundering the Hessian camp, at about six o'clock in the afternoon, a large force of the enemy, under Colonel Brayman, came suddenly upon them. They had been sent by Burgoyne as a reinforcement for Baum. Although his men were tired out by the former battle, Stark rallied his troops and again ordered an attack. After a short but very severe engagement, during which he was reinforced by a company of Green Mountain Boys under Warner, the enemy were compelled to retreat, leaving behind all their artillery.

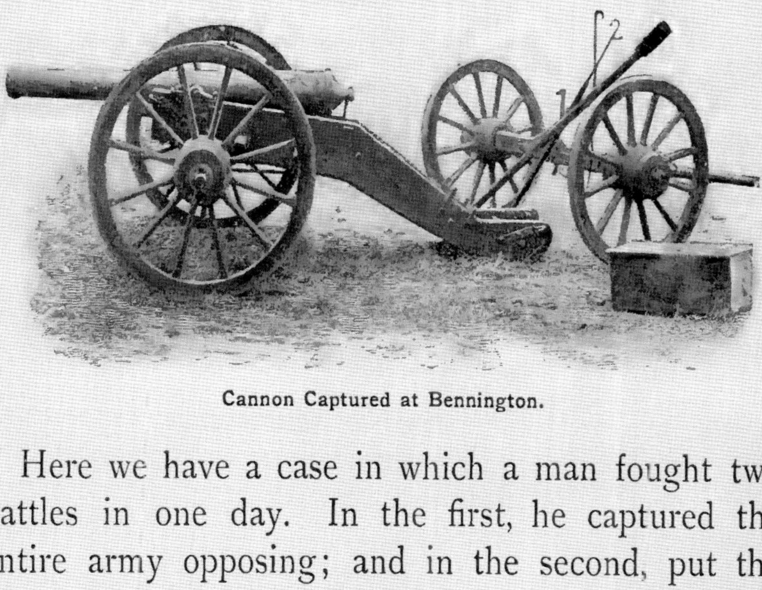

Cannon Captured at Bennington.

Here we have a case in which a man fought two battles in one day. In the first, he captured the entire army opposing; and in the second, put the enemy to rout. The following is an extract of Stark's account of the battle, forwarded by a messenger to the legislature of New Hampshire:

"Our people behaved with the greatest spirit and bravery imaginable. Had they been Alexanders or Charles of Sweden, they could not have behaved better. The action lasted two hours, at the expiration of which time we forced their breastworks at the muzzles of their guns, took two pieces of brass cannon, with a number of prisoners; but before I could get them into proper form again, I received intelligence that there was a large reinforcement within two miles of us on their march, which occa-

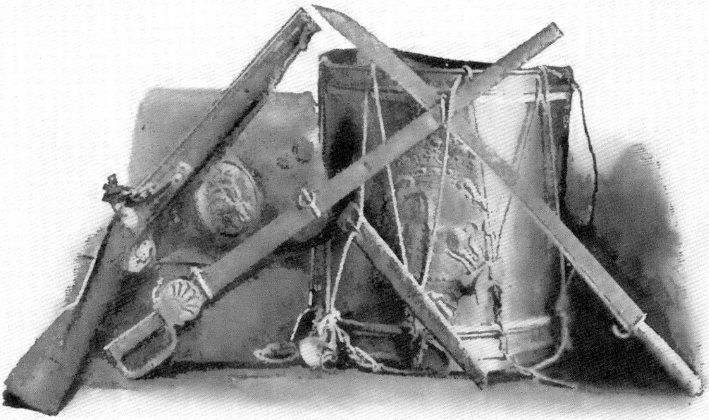

War Relics of Battle of Bennington.

sioned us to renew our attack. But lucky for us, Colonel Warner's regiment came up, which put a stop to their career.

"Soon we rallied, and, in a few minutes, the action began very warm and desperate, which lasted until night. We used their own cannon against them, which proved of great service to us. At sunset we obliged them to retreat a second time. We pursued them until dark, when I was obliged to halt for fear of killing my own men in the darkness. With one more hour of daylight, we would have captured the whole body. We recovered two pieces more of their cannon, together with all their baggage, a number of horses, carriages, etc., and killed upwards of two hundred of the enemy in the field of battle. The number of wounded is not yet known, as they are scattered about in many places. I have one lieutenant-colonel, since dead, one major, seven captains, fourteen lieutenants, four ensigns, two cornets, one judge-advocate, one baron, two Canadian officers, six sergeants, one aid-de-camp, one Hessian chaplain, three Hessian servants and seven hundred prisoners.

Signed, JOHN STARK,
Brigadier-General."

The effect of this victory was electrical. It was the first link of a chain of victories which led to the overthrow of the British. After the reverses of our army in Pennsylvania, it aroused the entire country to new hope. Recruits came pouring in.

When news of the battle was brought to Washington, he exclaimed, "One more such stroke, and we shall have no great cause for anxiety as to the future designs of Britain." Congress, when the news came, was about to "read New Hampshire out of the Union," but, instead, this resolution was passed:—

"Resolved, that the thanks of Congress be presented to General Stark of the New Hampshire militia, and the officers and troops under his command, for their brave and successful attack upon, and their signal victory over the enemy in their lines at Bennington; and that Brigadier Stark be appointed brigadier-general in the army of the United States." Years afterwards, President Jefferson wrote General Stark a letter in which he stated that the battle of Bennington was the culminating point in the fortunes of the colonists.

Burgoyne, having advanced beyond Ticonderoga, had placed his reliance upon foraging parties like Baum's to bring in provisions. The battle of Bennington proved that this was impossible, and his forces were thus cut off from all supplies.

Stark remained a month at Bennington and then rejoined General Gates at Bemis Heights, but the enlistment of his men having expired he returned with them to New Hampshire. In a short time he was given a larger command, and he now carried out his former policy of harassing Burgoyne's rear and of preventing any supplies reaching him from Canada. By this means he became an important factor in the final surrender of Burgoyne.

Stark Given Command of the Northern Department. —In the campaign of 1778, Stark was given the command of the northern department with headquarters at Albany. It was a difficult position, for while there was not much hard fighting, the country was full of Tories, who needed constant watching.

Later, he was ordered to join General Gates in Rhode Island, where he was engaged in reconnoitering the coast. When Gates went to New Jersey to reinforce Washington, Stark accompanied him, but the army soon went into winter quarters, and Stark returned home to raise recruits and supplies for the spring campaign.

It was with great difficulty that the New Hampshire legislature could be prevailed upon to provide sufficient clothing for their soldiers. One of the members of this body, named Ephraim Adams, an old campaigner in the French and Indian War, repeatedly called the attention of the legislature to their negligence in this direction, but his words produced little or no effect. Finally, on a bitterly cold winter's day, the old man arose, and in a most impressive manner thus addressed the legislature:—"Gentlemen, our soldiers are in the field fighting for the protection of our homes and families, and I would move, Mr. President, that they be allowed the privilege of growing wool upon their backs to protect them from the bitter cold." It is said that from this time on the New Hampshire soldiers were the best clothed regiments in the army.

In May Stark returned to New Jersey, and was present at the battle of Springfield, but he soon went back to New Hampshire for more recruits. He had such success that he was able in a short time to take reinforcements to West Point, where he left them, while he joined the army at Morristown. After Arnold's treachery, Stark was ordered to relieve General St. Clair at West Point, and to serve on the court-martial of Major André.

In 1781 Stark was again given the command of the northern department and stationed at Saratoga, where he was occupied principally with police duties, as the country was overrun with spies and traitors, and as robberies were of frequent occurrence. After the surrender of Cornwallis Stark dismissed the militia, and thanked them for their bravery and loyalty. He then returned to New England by way of Albany, and spent the winter in raising troops for the campaign of 1782. His long years of exposure had brought on a severe attack of rheumatism, and he was no longer able to take the field himself, but he did all in his power to aid the cause of liberty.

In appearance Stark was a man of medium size, well proportioned, and of great strength and endurance. It is remarkable that in all his years of hard service and in his many severe battles, he had never received a wound. In character he was kind, honest, frank and hospitable. He died at the advanced age of ninety-four, and was buried at Manchester, New Hampshire. After his death, there was left but one general who had taken part in the Revolutionary War.

CHAPTER IX.

GENERAL JOHN SULLIVAN.

Sullivan's Boyhood. — General Sullivan's father came from the province of Munster, Ireland, and settled in New England. Being well educated, he became a schoolmaster and taught the schools of Berwick, Maine, and of Somersworth, New Hampshire, until he was ninety years of age.

Sullivan's mother was also an emigrant from Ireland. When on the voyage, a passenger in a joking way asked her, "What do you expect to do in America?" "Do?" was the reply, "why, raise governors for them, sure." One of her sons was afterwards governor of Massachusetts, a grandson was governor of Maine, another a senator from New Hampshire, and yet another was lieutenant-governor of Illinois.

John was born at Somersworth, February 17, 1740. He received from his father what was then considered a very good education. When only a lad, he went on a voyage to the West Indies. On his return, he applied to Judge Livermore of Portsmouth for work, who, seeing before him a plain country boy clad in rough homespun, asked, "What can you do if I take you?" "Oh, I can split the wood, take care of the horse, attend to the gardening, and, perhaps, find

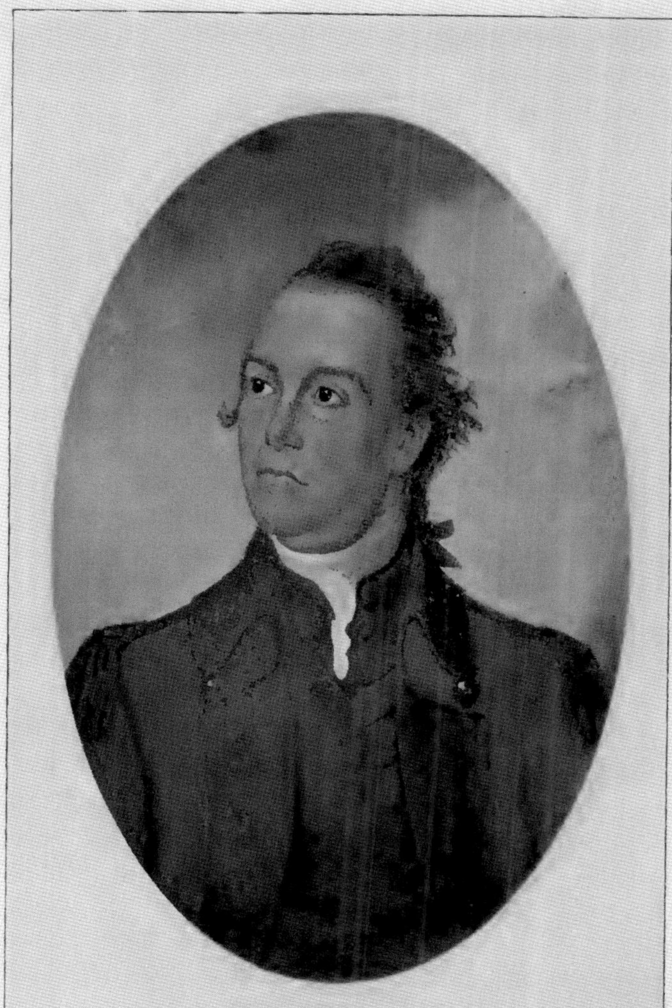

General John Sullivan.

some spare time to read a little, if you can give me that privilege," replied the boy. The judge was so pleased with his manner that he gave him a trial.

Mr. Livermore had an excellent library, and John improved every opportunity for study. One day, while the judge was away and Sullivan was reading in the library, a young man entered who had been accused of assault, and who wished to engage Judge Livermore to defend him. On learning that the judge was absent, he asked young John if he would not take the case. This he consented to do, and followed his client into court, which was then in session. In the meantime the judge came home, and, hearing that John had gone to the trial, followed to the court-room and slipped in silently to hear his manner of conducting the case. The prosecution showed the black and blue marks and enlisted the sympathies of all present. The case seemed against the boy, but he was able to prove that his client had received sufficient provocation, and the man was acquitted. The judge, greatly pleased, left as secretly as he had come. The next morning he sent for the lad and said, "John, the kitchen is no place for you, continue in your studies, give them your undivided attention, and you shall have what assistance you need from me until you are in a condition to repay it."

Experience as a Lawyer. — At the age of twenty, John Sullivan was married, and opened a law office in Durham. At this time there were but two lawyers in the entire province of New Hampshire. The profession was not considered very highly, and as a result the citizens resented young Sullivan's attempt to settle among them. They even gathered one bright evening about his house and threatened to tear it down unless he promised to leave. Sullivan addressed the angry people from an upper window and proposed to test the question by "single combat." It was decided, however, that he was so strong that no fitting opponent could be found, when James Sullivan, afterwards governor of Massachusetts, volunteered in his brother's place. In the battle which followed, James was victor, and John lived to bring honor and glory to the town of Durham.

During the exciting times just before the revolution, Sullivan took an active part, and in the spring of 1774 represented New Hampshire in Congress.

John Adams, in his diary, wrote as follows regarding the action taken by this Congress:—"The committee of violations of rights reported a set of articles which were drawn by Mr. John Sullivan of New Hampshire, and these two declarations . . . were two years afterwards recapitulated in the Declaration of Independence on the Fourth of July, 1776." Thus Sullivan played an important part in framing the Declaration which gave to America her independence.

Capture of Fort William and Mary.—On December 13 Paul Revere, the famous patriot of Boston, who afterwards brought news to Lexington, came to Sullivan with the announcement that the king had prohibited the importation of arms or military stores into the colonies, and that two regiments were about to march from Boston to occupy the fort near Portsmouth Harbor. To Sullivan's mind, the time had come for action. He quickly assembled a company of men, and on the following night, which happened to be clear and cold, they sailed down the river to Portsmouth, where half a dozen patriots were taken on board, among whom was Captain John Langdon, afterwards the first president of the United States Senate and governor of New Hampshire.

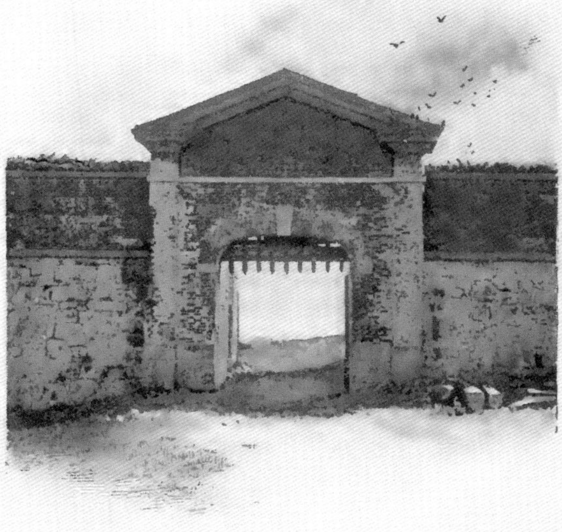

Portcullis of Fort William and Mary.

From Portsmouth they proceeded directly to the fort. The water was so shallow where they attempted to land, that they were forced to wade to the shore. Although bitterly cold, the men removed their shoes in order to make no noise while climbing the ramparts. The garrison, however, was alarmed, and made a sharp but unsuccessful resistance.[1]

The captain of the fort, together with his men, was seized and bound. They found here nearly two hundred kegs of powder, which they loaded on board their vessel and then proceeded back to Durham, where the powder was buried under the pulpit of the old meeting-house, as a means of security, for in those days no form of heating was used in church.

At the battle of Bunker Hill, the American troops were very short of powder. A modern writer has described their condition in the following manner:

"As the British were forming for a final charge on the earthworks, Prescott discovered that his men had hardly one round of ammunition. Dismayed at this, he gave the order to retreat. Undoubtedly both his forces and Stark's would have been captured except for the tremendous fire which Stark, from behind the rail fence, stuck with hay, was able to pour upon the Welsh fusileers who were marching to cut off the

[1] There is another account of the capture of Fort William and Mary, which gives the credit of its seizure to a band of Portsmouth citizens. They were said to have made an attack in broad daylight, and to have seized the fort without resistance on the part of its inmates.

The account as given in the text seems, however, to have the better historical support.

retreat. This Stark was able to do by a store of powder which came at a most opportune moment. It had been brought over the hills from New Hampshire, sixty miles away, by Captain John Demerritt in an ox-cart, and was a portion of the British powder captured at Portsmouth on the memorable 14th of December."

The news of Sullivan's assault upon the king's fortress was received with the greatest excitement in England. Parliament practically adopted a declaration of war, which was presented on February 9, 1775. The king promised "to uphold its wishes and that his language should open the eyes of the deluded Americans." Orders were immediately sent from London to seize all arms and ammunition to be found in the colonies, and Pitcairn's march to Lexington was the result. Dr. Quint of Dover, speaking of this attack, writes as follows: "The daring character of this assault cannot be overestimated. It was an organized investment of a royal fortress where the king's flag was flying, and the king's garrison met them with muskets and artillery. It was four months before Lexington, and Lexington was resistance to attack, while this was deliberate assault."

Alexander Scammel was in the expedition against Fort William and Mary, and it was he who hauled down the British flag. Scammel was one of Washington's closest friends, and later became adjutant-general of the entire army of the Revolution. He was killed during the siege of Yorktown, just before the surrender of Cornwallis; thus having taken part in the first and last struggle for independence. It is important for New Hampshire people to remember that this attack upon Fort William and Mary was the first armed resistance in the War of Independence, and that it took place four months before the battle of Lexington.

Governor Wentworth immediately issued a proclamation declaring all who had taken part in this attack guilty of treason, and offered a reward for their capture. Major Sullivan and other citizens of Durham who held commissions, either civil or military, from the king, marched boldly in a procession to the common, and there publicly burned their commissions, uniform, and everything that bound them to the king's service.

In order to defend his action in attacking the fort, Sullivan published an address, which was spread throughout the country, and from which this extract is taken: "I am far from wishing hostilities to commence on the part of America; but still hope that no person will, at this important crisis, be unprepared to act in his own defense, should he, by necessity, be driven thereto. And I must beg leave to recommend to the consideration of the people on this continent, whether, when we are by an arbitrary decree prohibited the having arms and ammunition by importation, we have not, by the law of self-preservation, a right to seize upon those within our power, in order to defend the liberties which God and nature have given us; especially at this time, when several of the colonies are involved in a dangerous war with the Indians, and must, if this inhuman order have the desired effect, fall a prey to those savages and barbarians, who have so often deluged this land with blood."

Sullivan Made Brigadier-General. — When the news of the battles of Lexington and Concord was received, Sullivan marched with his company to Massachusetts; but in May he resumed his seat in Congress and was appointed chairman of the war committee. At the time Washington was made commander-in-chief, eight brigadier-generals were appointed, and Sullivan was one of those to receive a commission. He went with his commander to Cambridge, and was stationed at Winter Hill during the siege of Boston.

After the victory, March 17, 1776, Sullivan was given command of the army in Canada. Upon arriving at his post, he found the army hungry and disheartened. Five thousand of the men were sick, and only about two thousand fit for duty. The enemy's forces were much stronger and in better condition. Under such circumstances there was nothing to do but to retreat. This retreat was conducted with such skill, prudence, and energy that the Americans were able to bring off all their sick, together with their guns and ammunition, the men dragging the cannon by hand through the wilderness.

Capture of Sullivan. — In August, Sullivan was made a major-general, and ordered to join Washington at New York. During the battle of Brooklyn, he was stationed at Brooklyn Heights, where with four thousand men he successfully opposed a much larger force of Hessians. He was able to hold his ground from nine o'clock until noon, when, being attacked upon the rear by forces outnumbering his own six to one, he was overpowered and captured while bravely leading a charge.

Sullivan was taken on board Lord Howe's flagship, the "Eagle," where he was kindly treated. During his captivity he was released on parole by Howe in order to take a message to Philadelphia, asking Congress to appoint a committee who should confer with him concerning terms of peace. This idea was carried out and the conference was held, but the committee came to no agreement, as they were not satisfied with Lord Howe's terms. General Sullivan was afterwards exchanged for General Prescott.

Sullivan at Trenton. — On regaining his liberty Sullivan joined the army under General Lee at North Castle, New York. Lee had been ordered to hasten to the relief of Washington, but he delayed and was captured by the enemy. Sullivan succeeded to the command, and lost no time in joining his forces with those of Washington beyond the Delaware. He arrived in time to take charge of the right wing in the battle of Trenton, and Colonel Stark was given command of the advance guard, which division conducted itself with such honor that Washington asked, "What troops are those?" General Sullivan replied, "Full-blooded Yankees, sir, from New Hampshire." It is said that Stockman Sweat, one of the "full-blooded Yankees" in Stark's regiment, distinguished himself by bringing in, unaided, five Hessian prisoners in a body. His explanation of the capture was that he did it by "surrounding them."

The time for which Sullivan's men had enlisted expired on the first of January, and as the enemy was approaching with a large force it was important to keep all the army together in order to prevent their advancing on Philadelphia; accordingly, he prevailed on his troops to reënlist for six weeks, thus making possible the victory of Princeton.

On the 13th of February, 1777, he wrote to Meshech Weare, president of the assembly of New Hampshire:—

"You may want to know how your men fight. I tell you, exceedingly well when they have the proper officers. I have been much pleased to see a day approaching to try the difference between Yankee cowardice and southern valor. The day, or rather the days, have arrived. . . . General Washington made no scruple to say, publicly, that the remnant of the eastern regiments was the strength of his army, though their numbers, comparatively speaking, were small. He calls them in front when the enemy are there; he sends them to the rear when the enemy threatens that way. All the general officers allow them to be the best of the troops. The southern officers and soldiers allow it in time of danger, but not at all at other times. Believe me, sir, the Yankees took Trenton before the other troops knew anything of the matter. More than that, there was an engagement; and, what will surprise you still more, the line that attacked the town consisted of but eight hundred Yankees, and there were sixteen hundred Hessians to oppose them. At Princeton, when the Seventeenth Regiment had thrown thirty-five hundred southern militia into confusion, a regiment of Yankees restored the day."

Battle of Brandywine.—Sullivan was given command of the right wing in the battle of Brandywine. The day on which the battle occurred was so foggy that the Americans had not been able to perceive the enemy's movements clearly, but it was reported that two brigades had crossed the Brandywine and were marching down the left bank. Washington ordered Sullivan to join the divisions of Stirling and Stephen in opposing the advance of the British. Upon his arrival, he found that instead of two brigades, the whole force of General Howe's army had crossed the river under cover of the fog.

The enemy began their attack before the Americans had time to form in line of battle, thus throwing many of them into confusion. The artillery, however, promptly took possession of a hill, and by their rapid firing kept the attention of the enemy until the broken troops could be rallied. General Sullivan behaved most courageously, at one time rallying the frightened soldiers, again directing the artillery on the hill, and exposing himself to every danger. His horse was shot under him during the engagement. Finally, by force of numbers, he was compelled to retreat, leaving the ground covered with the bodies of the enemy. Thus did three or four thousand American soldiers keep twelve thousand British at bay for nearly two hours, and then retreated in such good order that the enemy did not attempt to follow them.

In spite of the defeat at Brandywine, Washington resolved to again give battle to the British, but a violent storm destroyed his ammunition, and he was obliged to let Lord Howe enter Philadelphia unmolested. Howe quartered most of his soldiers at Germantown, eight miles north of Philadelphia. The Americans made a spirited attack upon this town, but on account of a dense fog which prevented their distinguishing friend from foe, they were forced to retreat.

Sullivan at Rhode Island. — General Sullivan spent the winter among the privations of Valley Forge. In April, 1778, he was given command of the army in Rhode Island. Upon arriving at Providence, he found his command reduced to only five hundred men; but, fortunately, the English, who were stationed at Newport under General Piggott, had no idea that they were opposed by so small a force.

Sullivan made every endeavor to increase the size of his army, which finally, after he was joined by the forces of Lafayette, numbered about ten thousand men. He was also aided by the French fleet under Count D'Estaing, but soon the French forces were withdrawn, which so disheartened the American troops that many deserted. Sullivan, being thus reduced in numbers, retreated at night to Butt's Hill, where he was attacked by the British. The battle lasted the entire day, and resulted in a complete victory for the Americans. Lafayette is reported to have said that Butt's Hill was the best fought battle of the war. The Americans lost but one hundred men, while the British lost over a thousand. Soon after, the British were heavily reinforced, and Sullivan was compelled to retreat. The legislatures of both New Hampshire and Rhode Island complimented General Sullivan upon his management of this campaign.

Expedition against the Iroquois. — The Iroquois Indians, who occupied the central part of New York State, were allies of the British, and had given much trouble to the Americans, so much so that Washington determined to teach them a lesson, and selected General Sullivan as a proper officer to inspire in them a respect for the American arms. Accordingly, in July, 1779, a small and poorly equipped army started up the Susquehanna River through the trackless wilderness to subdue a force of over a thousand Indians, together with seven or eight hundred British regulars.

At one time, when on the march, Sullivan's devotion to duty was clearly shown by his giving up his favorite charger as a pack horse, in order that necessary supplies should not be left behind.

On the 29th of August, scouting parties reported to Sullivan that a large force of Indians, Tories, and British soldiers under the command of the Indian, Joseph Brant, and of Colonel Butler, had entrenched themselves in a very strong position, and were awaiting the American advance.

It was a critical period, as the defense represented the entire fighting force of the Iroquois. Sullivan immediately formed his plan of attack; the artillery, well supported by infantry, were placed along the center, while the New Hampshire brigade, under Colonel Poor, crossed the swamp and fought their way stubbornly up the hill, which stood on the enemy's left, in order to flank their position. In spite of all opposition, the flank movement was successful, and the enemy being unable to withstand the combined attacks of the

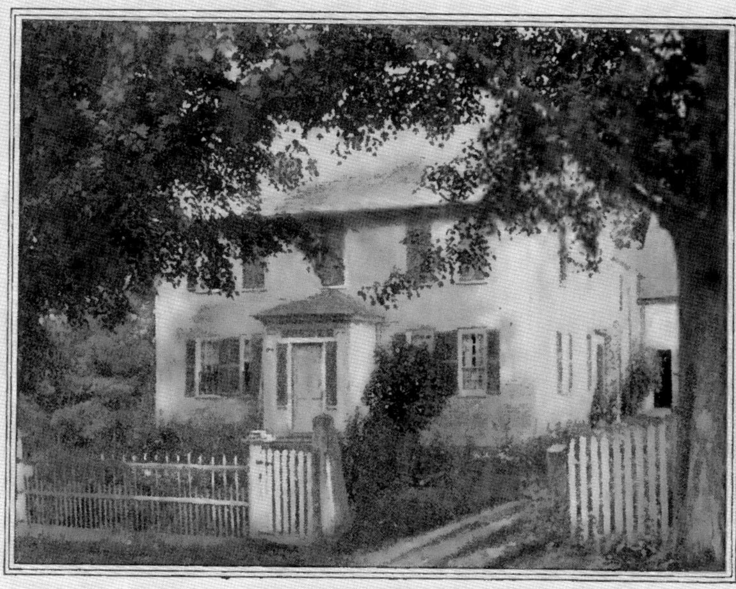

The Sullivan House.

artillery in front and of the infantry on their left, broke and fled.

The Indians were so impressed with the power of the Continental troops that they dared not risk another encounter, and the whole country was deserted. Sullivan, to make his conquest more complete, burned everything which could possibly be of use to the Indians.

On the 16th day of September the army arrived at Geneseo, the largest town of the Iroquois, which

Sullivan describes as consisting of one hundred twenty-eight large, elegant dwellings, with orchards of fine fruit trees, some of which were very old; also with large fields of corn and vegetables.

When he had completed the destruction of every village and cornfield belonging to the Five Nations, Sullivan began his return journey. The army arrived in Boston on the 15th of October, after a march of nearly seven hundred miles through the wilderness.

In recognition of the success of this expedition, Washington officially "congratulated the army on the complete and full success of Major-General Sullivan and of the troops under his command against the Senecas and other tribes of the Five Nations, as a just and necessary punishment for their wanton depredations, their unparalleled and innumerable cruelties, and their deafness to all entreaties." Congress also accorded a vote of thanks to Washington and Sullivan for the plan and successful issue of this expedition.

Sullivan Fills Many Important Positions. — Sullivan's health became so broken from his five years of hard service, that he was compelled to resign his commission. Congress accepted his resignation and expressed its gratitude for his valuable services. He reached Durham in February, 1780, anxious to resume his interrupted law practice and to quietly enter into private life. The people, however, had such trust in his integrity that they insisted on sending him as a delegate to Congress to present their New Hampshire side in the dispute over what is now Vermont, but which was then known as the "New Hampshire Grants." This controversy was not finally settled until 1791, when Congress decided to make the land into a separate state. Sullivan was also elected to hold the position of attorney-general for New Hampshire, which office was afterwards held by both his son and grandson.

Upon the retirement of Meshech Weare, General Sullivan was elected to the office of president of the state. When in the president's chair, Sullivan was very active in the support of the state military organizations, and formed twenty thousand militia into regiments of infantry, cavalry and artillery.

The Exeter Riot. — After the close of the war, the country was in a very demoralized condition. The people had expected that when they obtained their liberty, prosperity would come of its own accord. Many of them, therefore, as they still experienced the hard times, became clamorous for state aid. The trouble finally culminated at Exeter, where several hundred armed men assembled in open rebellion and demanded of the legislature that it should pass such laws as they wished. Among others, the following demands were most prominent; that there should be a large issue of paper money, that property should be equally distributed among all people, and, finally, that all debts should be abolished.

The mob assembled before the doors of the state house and threatened to use force unless the legislature granted their requests. Sullivan, who was president of the senate as well as of the state, stepped to the doors and addressed the rioters. He explained to them carefully wherein their claims were unjust, and told them that even if they were just, the legislature would not take any action while its members were threatened by an armed force.

The mob then left the building, but placed sentries at the door to prevent the senators from going home. Meantime, the senate proceeded with their customary business and adjourned at the usual hour. As Sullivan attempted to leave the chamber, the mob which had assembled barred his passage, and the cry arose from among them to fire upon him. Sullivan told them that he had already smelt too much powder to be afraid of theirs. At this moment a drum was heard in the distance, and the mob, thinking the artillery was coming, hastily withdrew. The next morning several companies of militia, including a squadron of cavalry, were drawn up in the town ready for action. At first the insurgents were disposed to resist, but being charged upon by the cavalry, they scattered in all directions. Several of the ringleaders were afterwards arrested, but, through the leniency of Sullivan, were discharged.

Final Adoption of the Constitution.—Sullivan played a very important part in the final adoption of the Constitution of the United States. It was necessary to have nine states agree to the Constitution before it could go into effect. Eight states had already voted in its favor, and it was of the greatest importance that New Hampshire should also give its sanction in order to have it adopted. Sullivan exerted all his influence in its favor, and on the 21st of June, 1788, New Hampshire adopted the Constitution by a vote of fifty-seven to forty-six. This date is important as it represents the adoption of the Constitution of the United States.

Washington, in 1789, appointed Sullivan United States Judge of New Hampshire, which office he held for many years.

During the latter part of his life, Sullivan suffered much from a spinal trouble brought on by an injury received in the Iroquois campaign. This caused his death on the 23d of January, 1795. He was buried in the little family cemetery near his home at Durham.

Upon the adoption of the Constitution the history of New Hampshire as a separate colony became merged into that of the United States, and consequently the sphere of this work has reached its limit.

During the years that have elapsed since the forming of the Union, New Hampshire has done her part toward moulding the destinies of the Republic. The names of Daniel Webster, Franklin Pierce, Salmon P. Chase, Horace Greeley, Henry Wilson, William Pitt Fessenden, Benjamin F. Butler, John P. Hale, Lewis Cass, John A. Dix, and Charles A. Dana recall the fact that a state small in area and in population may be great in the character of her men.

At one time, when Webster was asked to account for the "Great Stone Face" at Franconia, he made the following reply: "You merchants of the city display signs outside your doors to indicate what goods you make there; the Almighty has placed his sign on that cliff to indicate that he makes men here."

INDEX.

ADVERTISEMENTS

STORIES FROM ENGLISH HISTORY

EDITED BY

ALBERT F. BLAISDELL.

Square 12mo. Boards. 191 pages. Fully illustrated.
For introduction, 40 cents.

THIS is a book of stories from English history, edited for school and home use. It is intended to serve as a supplementary reading book for boys and girls from ten to fifteen years of age. It consists of a series of dramatic and notable events in English history from the earliest time to the present day, carefully compiled and rewritten from standard books and well-known authors.

The material has been arranged in the form of stories with the intent to arouse a lively interest in historical reading and a keen desire to know more about the history of our mother country.

It has been the aim of the editor to furnish in a readable and connected form a useful and convenient introduction to more advanced works for young folks on similar subjects.

It is needless to say that some of the stories, so far as historical accuracy is concerned, rest upon very slender foundations. Whatever semi-mythical character may be attached to these and other familiar stories in this book does not detract of course from the pleasure and instruction which they may afford youthful readers.

These stories, supplemented with various picturesque anecdotes, are written purposely in an easy and familiar style and in very simple language, with the aim to attract and hold the attention of young pupils.

GINN & COMPANY, Publishers,

Boston. New York. Chicago. Atlanta. Dallas.

CLASSICS FOR CHILDREN

Choice Literature; Judicious Notes; Large Type; Firm Binding; Low Prices.

For the prices and bibliography of these books, see our High School and College Catalogue.

Aesop's Fables.
Andersen's Fairy Tales. First Series.
Andersen's Fairy Tales. Second Series.
Bunyan's Pilgrim's Progress.
Burt's Stories from Plato.
Chesterfield's Letters.
Church's Stories of the Old World.
Defoe's Robinson Crusoe.
Dickens' Tale of Two Cities.
Cervantes' Don Quixote of La Mancha.
Epictetus.
Fiske-Irving's Washington and His Country.
Francillon's Gods and Heroes.
Franklin: His Life by Himself.
Goldsmith's Vicar of Wakefield.
Grimm's Fairy Tales, Part I.
Grimm's Fairy Tales, Part II.
Grote and Ségur's Two Great Retreats.
Hale's Arabian Nights.
Hatim Taï.
Hudson and Lamb's Merchant of Venice.
Hughes' Tom Brown at Rugby.
Irving's Alhambra.
Irving's Sketch-Book. (Six Selections.)
Johnson's Rasselas.
Kingsley's Greek Heroes.
Kingsley's Water Babies.
Lamb's Adventures of Ulysses.
Lamb's Tales from Shakespeare.
Marcus Aurelius.
Martineau's Peasant and the Prince.
Montgomery's Heroic Ballads.
Plutarch's Lives.
Ruskin's King of the Golden River.
Selections from Ruskin.
Scott's Guy Mannering.
Ivanhoe.
Lady of the Lake.
Lay of the Last Minstrel.
Marmion.
Old Mortality.
Quentin Durward.
Rob Roy.
Tales of a Grandfather.
Talisman.
Southey's Life of Nelson.
Swift's Gulliver's Travels.
White's Natural History of Selborne.
Williams and Foster's Selections for Memorizing.
Wyss' Swiss Family Robinson.

GINN & COMPANY, PUBLISHERS,

Boston. New York. Chicago. Atlanta. Dallas.